A RENOVATED LIFE

Restoration Room by Room

Kit Roberts

Dedicated to my husband, Gary,
and my son, Tyler,
who witnessed the worst in me
and chose to see the best in me!

Thank you for always loving me!

Contents

Foreword

I read Kit's book in one sitting. It is an incredibly courageous and very generous gift to the world. She compares the process of renovating a house to that of recovering from a substance use disorder, and the analogy works! She speaks of building the foundation and making sure it's solid, installing a front door that can be sturdy enough to keep out unwanted strangers, but also welcoming enough to invite friends to pass over the threshold. She writes about the kitchen, the bathroom, the attic and has lovely stories to illustrate each of these critical rooms, and she describes the importance of having a serene place to retreat and a "prayer chair" for times when she just needs to be alone. She even draws analogies between the importance of having the right construction tools for each job and the right tools of recovery for each person's particular recovery journey.

Kit struggled to get sober for 15 years after attending her first AA meeting, so this is not a quick, sanitized, airbrushed version of recovery. No, Kit manages to write about the difficult process of recovery with clear-eyed honesty, humor, tenderness, authenticity, and even grace.

I believe that anyone who is struggling to reinvent, renovate or renew their life will benefit from reading this sweetly courageous book about becoming sober and re-engaging with the world, one step at a time, and one room at a time.

The very first time I met Kit she was sitting next to me in our small connect group (think "grown up Sunday School") that meets on Sundays prior to the worship service at our church. She turned to me and said warmly, "I hear you're a coach. I'm thinking of quitting my job and going into coaching and I'd love to talk to you about what you do." I remember thinking to myself at the time what a bright, shiny star of a person she was, with glistening dark eyes, platinum streaks in her thick hair, and a palpable hyper-kinetic personality that immediately made me want to learn more about her.

After this initial meeting, Kit, and I and two other women formed a small Bible study group and started meeting every other week at her comfy home, filled with inspiring quotes and cozy spaces. She said that she wanted and needed friends and so she took the bull by the horns and invited us to join her at her home, and just like that we had a full-fledged friends' group, a safe and welcoming place where we could meet regularly in person to talk about life, struggles, joys, and our faith. We now have 7 sweet sisters in our group. It's a wonderful small community of woman who gather in person for sweet fellowship and connection – and Kit started it. She renovated her life by adding a large dose of community to it, and we all benefited.

From the very first moment I walked inside Kit's house I could tell that she was serious about making it a home. It's got an ultra-cozy modern farmhouse vibe, complete with inspirational quotes and all the right little touches that some women just know how to do instinctively. She made all of us women feel as if we were special and important from the very first time we met together, and we have all deepened our friendships because of Kit's special brand of hostessing.

As I first started to learn about Kit's road to recovery from substance abuse, I was both impressed and amazed at her wisdom, humility, and sometimes raucous humor, as she shared stories from times when she was "under the influence". Soon, I began to really look forward to our gatherings, just so I could hear what Kit was up to. I loved her vivacious spirit, sassy style, and sense of adventure. It was during one of our early visits at her home that Kit shared about a book she was starting to write, this very book you now hold in your hands. She told us that she wanted to use this book to share her story of hope and healing with the world and in this way try to make a difference for others who have also struggled to recover from addiction. Several months later, when Kit asked me if I wanted to write the foreword for this book, I said yes without giving it a second thought. Why on earth would I *not* want to write the opening words for my sweet friend's amazingly brave offering of herself?

To all of you who are reading this, yes, life is hard, but it is also beautiful and worthwhile. If we keep putting one foot in front of the other, we will slowly but surely make progress through the darkest despair and the most challenging times a person can face, and move into a life of meaning, purpose, peace, love, joy, and deeply cherished connections. Well done, my sweet and sassy friend, and may you continue to grow, learn, and teach what you have learned, as you take your beautiful book out into the world to make it a better place.

Rebecca Merrill, EdM, MSW

Preface

Hidden Potential

"Recovery is an acceptance that your life is in shambles and you have to change it."

~Jamie Lee Curtis

I once read that the human attention span is one second less than that of a goldfish. Read that sentence again. One second LESS!

Fortunately for you and me, that story was debunked. Whew! The misleading theory was gleaned from a Microsoft research team in 2015 when they reported that the average human attention span lags one second behind goldfish. Within hours, this news hit the headlines worldwide. The report even graced the pages of *Time Magazine*. In a world teeming with buzzing smartphones, flashing billboards, and the constant hum of information, it's tempting to believe that we are more easily sidetracked than ever before. It seems logical to connect distraction with a lack of focus.

Could it be possible that our fascination with "fixer upper" shows is related to this notion of our shortened attention spans? These shows are typically short and easy to follow, with a clear beginning, middle, and end. They also offer a sense of satisfaction as we watch the transformation of a dilapidated property into something beautiful. Just look at the line up on HGTV on any given day or check out Netflix and you quickly see that many of us can't get enough of these makeover shows. From *Good Bones* to *Property Brothers* to *Extreme Makeover: Home Edition*. Remember Ty Pennington shouting, "Bus driver, move that bus!" as he stood in front of a large crowd gathered to see one of the hometown heroes view their newly remodeled home? My personal, all-time favorite is *Fixer Upper,* starring Chip and Joanna Gaines. I love seeing the old made new!

We watch and wait with anticipation as the show reaches that magical moment known to us as "The Big Reveal!" We ooh and awe over all the shiny new additions that make the homeowners beam with happiness knowing this is their new "old" home. They exclaim with utter amazement they can hardly believe it's the same house. The viewer saw the home in its "before" state and is equally impressed with the changes. The home had a good foundation and so much hidden potential. It just needed a vision of what it could become. It needed help with what I call, the "in-betweens." You know, all the hard work that takes place between the initial "before" pictures to the spectacular "after" photos.

We live in a world that demands instant gratification. We want a quick fix to all our woes. Whether it's losing weight, a new job, better health, meaningful friendships, or lasting love. We want it easy. We want it fast. We want it now. Life renovations don't work like that. Perhaps that's why we're given a whole life to live to figure it out. To decide what we want our "in-betweens" to resemble. There's much to be learned in the "in-betweens" and a beautiful, renovated life to be lived in the process.

My brother-in-law, Mike, was a general contractor for over 30 years. In addition to building homes from start to finish, he also did numerous renovations–both big and small. I asked him which he preferred building, new homes or renovations and without skipping a beat he said, "New builds are better." He went on to explain that with any renovation project there is always the presence of the unknown. What looks like a relatively simple and inexpensive change can quickly turn into a huge project with unexpected costs associated with hidden flaws the owner of the home was unaware of when they decided to remodel. The worst project to take on is a remodel a homeowner starts and realizes a little too late the project is more than their DIY abilities allow.

There's much to be learned in the "in-betweens" and a beautiful, renovated life to be lived in the process.

Because these "fixer- upper" shows must be condensed to fit an allotted airtime, you only see snippets of the work involved in the remodel. You don't see the intense sweat involved in carefully tearing down walls to make a room bigger without dislodging the trusses that hold the roof in place. You are unable to experience the patience required by the homeowner when weather conditions delay the project. And you certainly don't feel the actual pain that comes with hitting your thumb with a hammer or the muscle aches that follow long hours of work. All of that is messy, and necessary, and hard. But without it... there would be no renovation.

For the renovation or remodel to be successful, the home needs a solid plan, the right tools in the right hands, and someone to guide the process to ensure the vision of the homeowner becomes a reality. Recovery needs that same precision. So many mistakes and misfortunes may have eclipsed your life in addiction that you may wonder if it's even worth it to attempt a renovation rehab and, if you dare try, where to begin? I speak from experience when I say it's worth every ache, every splinter, every sore muscle to renovate a life from one of addiction to one of recovery.

Even as I write this book, in my 59th year of life, I'm still a work in progress. Progress, not perfection. That's one of the many sayings in the rooms of 12 step meetings. I'm still trying to lose those unwanted 10 pounds. I attempt to slow the aging process by slathering my face with potions and lotions all claiming to take 10 years off my looks. I buy whitening toothpaste in hopes of creating a bright, white smile. I read books about creating good habits. I create Pinterest boards for healthy recipes. On and on goes the list. A work in progress, always.

I've had the desire to write this book for several years and now, here I sit at my computer, wondering if I can do it. Ideas have swirled around inside my head. I've made notes on my phone, I've written ideas in my journal, I've daydreamed of the day I will hold a copy of THIS book in my hands. I know the results I want but the tasks associated with getting there seem daunting at times. I feel overwhelmed–sometimes to the point of feeling paralyzed. I'm wondering if you can relate to this. The project seems too big. Like so many of us, I want it now. IG in my house doesn't stand for Instagram, it stands for "instant gratification" and I've been riddled with it most of my life.

However, I made the important decision this year to be patient. Or at least attempt to be because this is not who I am at my core. I am an impatient person. I don't wait well in lines. I may have just a smidgen of road rage when I get in traffic. Patience may be a virtue, but it is not one I currently possess.

I also deal with ADD. I think I've had it all my life, but it seems to have gotten worse during menopause. I can't point to any scientific research that indicates this to be true, it just seems everything gets worse with menopause!

I remember as a child there was a cartoon in the Sunday paper called, "The Family Circus." (I wonder how many of you reading this book even remember the "cartoon section" of the paper.) What memories I have of getting the Sunday morning paper after church and carefully opening it up to find the section marked "Comics." "Peanuts" by Charles Schulz held the headline for all the years I can remember reading the funny papers.

I'd get the paper and stretch out on my belly across the shag carpet of the living room floor, propping myself up on my tiny elbows as I started reading. First, "Peanuts" to see if Snoopy had yet been successful in beating the Red Baron or if Charlie Brown connected with the football before Lucy moved it away right before he tried to kick it. Next was "Blondie" to find out what sort of predicament Dagwood would find himself in or what he might find in the kitchen to eat. Then there was "Garfield" and finally, I'd land on "The Family Circus."

My favorite "Family Circus" cartoons were when little Jeffrey would be playing in the nearby playground and his mom would call him home. On his way home, Jeffrey would stop someone walking their dog so he could give it a quick pat on the head, then he'd jump into a puddle of water ensuring he was sufficiently covered in murky mud, followed by an abrupt stop to watch a line of ants hard at work building their anthill and several other stops marked by a dotted line on the paper indicating the path he took to get home. Even as a young child, I resonated with the distractions Jeffrey faced.

During my high school years, I described my inability to focus as a "butterfly with hiccups." That's how I felt my brain worked. If you envision a butterfly flitting from flower to flower, that alone is a jerky flight pattern. Now, add to that sight the poor insect having hiccups! Imagine how much more erratic the flight would be. Yet, somehow, with this undiagnosed condition, I managed to graduate high school, go on to college where I earned a degree in Communication Arts.

I don't have to tell you that life can be a struggle.

(And there, my dear reader, is a perfect example of the rabbit holes my brain chases! I think I was writing about the importance of patience and somehow managed to go off the rails with a story about "Family Circus.")

I don't have to tell you that life can be a struggle. If you've lived any number of years on this earth, you know it from experience as well. I share my stories of my imperfect impatience, the impact menopause has on my memory and focus and that even in recovery, I'm still a work in progress. I can still be insecure although I will tell you that with age does come wisdom, or maybe it's just that I am getting older and can't remember that I felt insecure.

Just a few months ago, I was driving into my neighborhood, wondering if I even had anything worth sharing in a book. I was thinking, *What do I know? What could I possibly share with someone else that might make a difference? What were you thinking, Kit?? You can't do this!* (Yes, I often have conversations with myself. I bet if you're honest, you do too!)

And then, my eyes filled with tears as I thought, *You have 10 years of sobriety, Kit. It took so many years to finally get it, but you never quit trying. That's worth something and worth sharing. There are bound to be other people, just like me, who desperately want to get sober, or make changes in their life and perhaps have lost hope. Yes, Kit… you can do this!*

In that moment, my circumstances didn't change but what I chose to believe about myself did. Now, every time I doubt my ability to finish this book, create a new habit, stick to an exercise program, or whatever change I want to make in my life, I remember it all begins with a choice. I can choose to say, "I can do this."

I can choose to say, "I can do this."

What about you? What aspect of your life are you looking at now that you think might need repair or remodeling? How do we know when we need to be renovated? Sometimes, like houses, things start falling apart and we recognize we need to make changes. We may not even know what those changes may be, but intuitively we know we can't continue on our current path. Sometimes a house gets a funny smell, or a squeak, or a slant, or things just start falling off the walls if a door is shut too hard. When the little things that are going wrong start adding up to big things, we know something needs to be fixed.

But how do we know what needs to be repaired unless we take a closer look? That's where the idea of soul-searching with regards to our own renovation begins. We recognize signs of dishevelment but aren't fully aware of what's causing it. Sometimes it's outward signs. Our health, our weight, or our skin reveals signs that something is wrong. Sometimes it's that internal ache of sadness, or longing, or discontentment that lets us know it's time to open our hearts and minds to discover the cause. Like a surgeon with a scalpel in hand, we need to carefully open the aching parts to discover the root cause.

My hope is that *A Renovated Life* will help you uncover or discover the parts of your life that need repair, whether large or small.

If I've learned nothing else in my nearly 60 years on this earth, it's that we just must begin. It means making a deliberate effort to do what is sometimes unnatural, or seemingly even impossible. The idea of writing this book had been in my heart for at least two years before I ever started. I might even speculate that it had been formulating in my head for years prior to the idea really gelling in my mind.

Many of us who find ourselves on the other side of recovery, want nothing more than for our story to help others. We hope our mess will one day be a message of hope and healing. Over the past few years, I've felt a strong sense that I needed to put some meat on the skeleton of my dreams. I had no idea what it would look like, but the desire to "begin" grew and grew. In my devotions one morning, I read a verse that spoke to me, telling me that it was time. I just needed to start. The verse was Psalms 32:8

"I will instruct you and teach you in the way you should go. I will counsel you with my loving eye on you."

If you're like me, you can spend so much time thinking about and planning what needs to be done that you fail to move forward. (In the South, we say we're "fixin' to do" something.) I finally made the decision to proceed–and knew that while yes, it was necessary to plan, (and I most definitely needed some type of blueprint, directions, guidance, or plan when I embarked on this renovation) at some point, I just needed to begin.

I realized with such clarity the moment I read that verse, that I had a General Contractor who indeed had a plan for my life and knew best. He held the original blueprint of my life in His hands and was ready not only to restore me to my original form, but He was going to rebuild and remodel those parts that had become rusty and worn. He would provide the instructions and oversee the project–I just had to begin.

I believe we all need some type of General Contractor to help us read the blueprint of our life; to read it and reshape it as needed.

My hope is this book will help you do just that. My hope is this book will offer you both wisdom and wit, based on the road of happy destiny I have traveled thus far.

So, take out whatever you need to help you on this journey whether it's graph paper, a journal, a notebook, pen and paper, or a computer program–whatever you need, and join me.... as you begin your own Renovated Life.

 **"Renovation Reflections"**

1. What surprises have you uncovered that now need attention in your recovery journey?

2. Who in your life is providing you with support, accountability, and/or guidance with your recovery?

3. What beliefs do you need to change about yourself to help you move forward successfully in your recovery journey?

Next: Let's begin by creating a blueprint, a detailed plan that allows you to focus on each step of recovery while keeping your long-term goal in sight.

Chapter 1

Design Your Purpose

"Sobriety was the greatest gift I ever gave myself."

~Rob Lowe

In a world where home renovations reign supreme, I think I can say with much confidence that no brave soul has ever ventured into the realm of total transformation without a solid plan. It's like attempting a wild adventure without a map—too many unknowns lie in wait, ready to pounce and turn your dreams into nightmares. Even the boldest builders, those with hammers in their hands and dreams in their hearts, would stare at you in disbelief if you dared to ask whether they'd construct a house without a blueprint. Trust me, it's a wild ride you don't want to take without a roadmap to guide you through the twists and turns of renovation madness!

A blueprint gives the contractor a picture of the finished project as well as all the materials and measurements needed to build it. It gives the builder a step-by-step process to follow. Adjustments can be made along the way to accommodate personal preferences, but having a guide makes the process much more manageable. Recovery can be viewed in much the same way.

Being the daughter of an Army father, we moved around quite a bit when I was a child. Towards the end of my father's military career, my parents purchased a house plan with the intention of building it when my father retired, and we moved back to their hometown. His father, while not an educated man, was a smart man. He and my grandmother opened a restaurant while my father was in high school. While neither of them had experience in the restaurant industry, my grandfather was a savvy businessman, and my grandmother was an extraordinarily good cook. It was a winning combination! The restaurant served up thousands of delicious meals, scrumptious desserts and created a loyal customer base for over 25 years. (Being in that restaurant holds some of the most cherished memories of my childhood.)

While my grandfather purchased a few luxury items for my grandmother, he used to say that no one was making any more land, recognizing that real estate was a smart investment. He didn't need a college education to know that. With the profits he made from "Redman's Café", he purchased several rental properties as well as almost 100 acres of fertile farmland all on the same curvy, country road on which they lived. My parents' plan was to build their dream home on those 100 acres.

I remember many times asking my mother to get the house plans out so I could look at them. They were held in the cardboard cylinder container in which they were mailed and kept tucked under my mom and dad's antique green painted double bed in their bedroom. (Antique green. Does that bring back memories for any of you? That bedroom set my mother "antiqued" with green paint and a gold overlay was solid cherry! What was she thinking?)

She would get them out for me, and I would carefully roll out the blueprints, studying them with a vivid imagination and daydreaming about the large bedroom with dormer windows that would eventually be mine. While I was unable to decipher the details of the blueprints, I could envision the home sitting on the piece of property we planned to build it on. It was a great way to muse what the future held after dad retired.

I've always enjoyed looking at house plans, lost in a world of possibilities, dreaming of the day I might build a home of my very own. There's an adage that claims if a marriage can endure the trials of building a house, it can withstand anything. Witnessing my parents embark on their own house-building journey, watching them stay committed through thick and thin, I was convinced I could do the same. However, my husband, Gary, remains unconvinced. For him, the practicality of purchasing an existing home far outweighed the allure of building from scratch.

Consider the countless decisions that go into constructing a home. It's not a mere matter of assembling walls according to a blueprint. No, it's the multitude of countless choices that give a home its unique character. From the intricate details of baseboards that grace *The list of detailed decisions can be daunting.* each room, to the style of cabinets that breathe life into the kitchen and bathrooms, to the delicate dance of doors, knobs, and windows—oh, my! The list of detailed decisions can be daunting. But it's those tiny details that give it a distinct personality. It's the personal preferences sprinkled throughout the new build that transform it from a mere house plan to that of an inviting home.

When embarking on a new build, a blueprint serves as the guidebook that can be tweaked and altered to suit the builder's needs and desires. Those alterations are best done by a skilled architect. Equipped with their training and experience, they possess the ability to assess and determine the feasibility of these modifications. I recall the home my parents had planned to construct on that sprawling hundred-acre plot, where they intended to settle after retiring from military service. The den, as it appeared in the original plans, fell a tad short of the desired measurements they envisioned. It was then that my father, ever the visionary, marked the dimensions of the room on the ground, straying four feet beyond the confines of the original blueprint. Such a change would inevitably affect the layout of the second story and the overall dimensions of the home. Armed with this new tangible vision, my father approached an architect, tasking them with the redesign of the blueprints to accommodate his alterations.

A blueprint is a sacred document that bridges the homeowner's dreams with the craftsmanship of the general contractor. It is through this blueprint that they examine together, assessing whether it meets the homeowner's needs and can be brought to life on the chosen plot of land. Yet, many homeowners find themselves bewildered by the multitude of measurements, numbers, and lines on the blueprint. It becomes necessary to seek the guidance of an expert, someone with the required skills to decipher this code, if you hope to see your vision materialize.

I don't know if people always think about having a blueprint, or at least a plan in place, when they start a renovation project. Simple renovations perhaps don't need one, but elaborate home remodeling projects are more successful when we have the outline of the necessary steps, the needed tools, and someone who can provide guidance along the way. The order in which things are done can be important when you begin a remodeling project. You don't want to lay new flooring first if you intend to tear down a wall, due to the mess involved in the teardown. Sometimes, when we know we want to change something, we dive in headfirst deciding we'll figure it out along the way. That's typically where some of the biggest renovation issues arise. Had we taken the time to plan the project, outlining the process, we may have avoided some mishaps. There's a reason why, in the world of building, you often hear, "measure twice, cut once."

Blueprints serve as a treasure trove of information for builders, offering detailed instructions on how to bring a building or structure to life. While the homeowner's primary interest lies in the floor plan, which reveals the home's layout, including room dimensions, window and door placements, and the arrangement of walls, there is additional information within the blueprint that holds more significance to the builder than the homeowner.

Can you see how building a life in recovery is a lot like building a new home and why sometimes we need to redesign the current build or renovate the original structure? Much like a blueprint provides a meticulously detailed plan for constructing a home, recovery from addiction demands a thoughtfully crafted roadmap. As you embark on this journey of recovery, crafting your own plan of action, you begin to identify potential stumbling blocks and problem areas that may impede your progress. Just as an architect can reshape a home's design through subtle or significant changes, it is vital to find someone in your life who can help identify triggers, problem areas, and guide you through the uncharted territories of recovery.

Remodeling a home, and all the intricacies that go with it, is not an overnight process. Often one small remodeling project leads to multiple ones. Recovery from addiction is a lifelong journey as well. Many changes are required during recovery and just when you think you've got one skill mastered, life throws you a fast ball, breaking windows, and shattering glass all over what you have just finished cleaning up. That's why we learn to "take life on life's terms." We'd prefer that once we get our house in order, it stays that way. But we know that's not the reality of the world in which we live.

Recovery from addiction is a lifelong journey as well.

While building a home, or making renovations to it, requires physical changes, recovery requires making changes to your behavior and thought patterns. Patience becomes a guiding force. Progress unfolds gradually, and it requires patience to traverse the ups and downs, to embrace the small victories, and to understand that lasting change takes time. Perseverance becomes the driving force that propels your recovery forward. The path to recovery can be challenging, marked by moments of doubt and the need to push through discomfort. Perseverance ensures that setbacks are not perceived as failures but rather as opportunities for growth and learning.

Maintaining a laser-like focus on the end goal is paramount. You must hold onto a vision of a healthier, more fulfilling life, utilizing it as a beacon of hope during moments of temptation or doubt. By staying focused on the goal of a life of sobriety, you begin to confidently navigate the difficulties of your journey with clarity and purpose.

Recovering from addiction requires a well-defined plan that emphasizes the present while maintaining a mindful eye on the future. Like a builder who meticulously attends to each stage of the construction process while envisioning the outcome, in recovery you must focus on each step of your plan while keeping your long-term goals, hopes, and dreams in sight. By staying fully present and dedicated to each phase of your recovery blueprint, you can construct a solid foundation, attain enduring success, and create a resilient spirit that withstands the obstacles and triggers surely to come your way.

 **"Renovation Reflections"**

1. What does your current blueprint for recovery look like?

2. How are you adapting your old life to your new life in recovery?

3. Who is helping you decipher the changes you may need to make to your current recovery blueprint?

Next: No structure can stand without a solid foundation. That means you must enlist aid from supporters who will stand by you and shore you up against weaknesses that will inevitably arise during recovery.

Chapter 2

Huff and Puff

"I got a message, a little thought, that said, 'Do you want to live or die?' I said I wanted to live. And suddenly the relief came, and my life has been amazing."

~ **Anthony Hopkins**

D o you remember the fable about the three little pigs? Whether we realize it or not, we were taught at a very early age through this story the importance of building with materials that would withstand some of the toughest "blows" life sends our way.

The story helps us understand the importance of a firm foundation. In case you're unfamiliar with the fictitious yarn, the basic storyline goes something like this: There are three little pigs whose mother sends them out into the world to make their fortune. (It must have been time for them to learn how to bring home the bacon!) The first two pigs are more interested in playing than in hard work, so they quickly build themselves a shelter using material they can secure from strangers passing by.

The first little pig secures bales of straw, and the second little pig builds his abode with bundles of sticks. (Maybe they were the first to build tiny homes!) But that third little pig, obviously the construction guru, builds his house out of strong bricks. Shortly after construction of all three homes was complete, a big, bad hungry wolf came sniffing outside the pig's respective residences. We learn quickly he's not a nice wolf and exhibits characteristics of a bully. Outside each of the little pig's homes, he bellows to the little pig to let him in. When he is refused entry, he ensues to "huff and puff" and blows down the houses made of straw and sticks, forcing the little pigs to run to the brick home of their brother. When that big bad wolf reaches the home of the third pig that built his home out of bricks, all the wolf's "huffing and puffing" is of no avail. The house built on the solid foundation of bricks and mortar was no match for the mean ol' wolf!

As an adult, I understand there are metaphorical life lessons to be gleaned from this fable, but I can't help but think about how scary this story must be to a child. A wolf trying to get into the home of those pigs and then blowing their house down! Kinda terrifying if you ask me. Let's face it, many of the fairy tales we baby boomers grew up with would never pass the "politically correct" test today! But what we see in the story of the "Three Little Pigs" is that not only do we need to learn to build well with material that will withstand the storms of life, but we see that the little pig whose house could withstand the harm the wolf was trying to inflict on his fellow piglets, opened his home to those that needed it. Even though the two little pigs had not planned well when selecting the material for building their home–maybe they cut corners because they were lazy or simply couldn't afford to buy bricks–the third pig shared his home willingly to help his brothers.

Another lesson subtly woven into this seemingly innocent fable is that life is going to have at least one Big Bad Wolf that wants to blow our house down and, after doing so, may try consuming us. In the very first edition of the "Three Little Pigs" the wolf ate the first and second pig. Yikes! I'm so glad someone decided to change that part of the original story. Can you imagine telling a young child the story that included the little pigs basically becoming BBQ or bacon for the furry, four-legged villain. Like I said, several of the fairy tales some of us grew up with were a bit sketchy!

However, at some point in our life, the wolf will be after us. It may be hiding in the woods, sniffing out our weaknesses, ready to jump on us when we least expect it. It may be circling our home at night, low on its haunches, creeping around the perimeter. Watching. Patiently waiting for just the right time to pounce. We all have at least one wolf. Many of us have faced a whole pack!

We all have at least one wolf.

The biggest, baddest wolf I've faced so far in my life was alcoholism and it consumed me for years.

One day, I'm going to write a different book about the years the wolf had me clenched tight in his mouth. During that time, I wasn't thinking of the house that he'd blown down to get to me. I wasn't thinking about the path of destruction he'd left in his wake as he gained access to me. I wasn't prepared for the fight. There were times I wished that mean ol' wolf would just finish me off rather than keep me alive–ever toying with me. In those years of captivity by the wolf, I didn't think rebuilding was possible. I didn't have a foundation. There seemed to be no solid ground on which to dig. Heck, even if I located land on which to start building, I didn't have a shovel to start digging or a plan on what to build.

A foundation is what holds a house in place. If the foundation is not level and laid with precision, the entire home can be compromised. Building a solid foundation is a lot like the game of Jenga. If you start with a shaky base, everything's going to come crashing down, the higher up you go. And when that happens, you don't want to be the one responsible for ruining game night.

If you've ever bought a home, one of the things that is required prior to purchasing it is a home inspection. The inspection will consist of several things. The inspector will examine the electrical wiring, all the wall outlets, and light fixtures to ensure they meet the required safety codes. They will also look at the plumbing system which includes the pipes, bathtubs, showers, toilets, and drains to see if there is any past damage or any current leaks that could lead to problems that really stink. They'll check the HVAC system, the roof, and even the appliances. If any issue is found, the inspector will include it in the report to the potential new homeowner to see if it needs to be fixed prior to purchase or if the home will be purchased "as is." While you hope the inspector doesn't find any defects in these systems, you know if he does, typically, there are remedies, or the possibility of renovations, to repair them.

But what you don't want to see in the inspector's final report are issues with the foundation. If the foundation is bad or off balance, a whole slew of serious structural issues could compromise the entire safety of the home. A poorly constructed foundation can cause walls, floors, and ceilings to crack or shift. An unstable foundation can cause the basement or crawl space to flood, leading to water damage which could, in turn, lead to the growth of mold and mildew. You know what kind of creepy crawlies like to live in a musty, damp environment, don't you? No thank you!

A foundation that is deemed structurally unsound may lead to potential repairs that can be complex and costly. A home buyer may decide not to move forward with the purchase of the home if problems with the foundation are reported. Foundational problems can be fixed but sometimes the cost isn't worth it. That's why it's so important to make sure the foundation is right from the start.

Just as a home built on a bad foundation is at risk of cracking, crumbling, or collapsing entirely, a life built on a weak foundation is fodder for the wolf. Without a strong start, we become susceptible to setbacks and challenges that may be difficult for us to overcome. It's important to invest time and effort into building a solid foundation of recovery. Thankfully, remodeling the foundation of our lives doesn't have to be as costly as repairing a literal foundation of a home, but the work involved can be just as difficult. You must be sure you're up for the task.

A firm foundation of recovery necessitates a solid support system. Surrounding yourself with understanding and compassionate individuals who believe in you and your desire to remodel your life is crucial. These supporters may be the barrier you'll need against the metaphorical "big bad wolf" of relapse. They can provide encouragement during moments of vulnerability.

When you build a firm foundation in recovery, you protect yourself from the destructive forces of addiction. A well-built recovery will withstand the huffing and puffing of the big bad wolf and equip you with strength and resilience. It is an ongoing process that requires dedication and vigilance, but the rewards of a healthier, happier life far outweigh the challenges faced along the way.

Yes, we learn early the repercussions of not building a structure that can withstand the storms life sends our way.

Yes, we learn early the repercussions of not building a structure that can withstand the storms life sends our way. And when those wolves or Jenga blocks or trials or whatever you want to call the unexpected, unpleasant circumstances enter our lives, we find we must face them. It's in facing them that we begin to see the opportunity for renewal and renovation.

So, let's take a lesson from those two pigs that didn't plan so well and begin with a firm foundation in recovery as we remodel our lives. You can do this! Grab your hard hat, lace up those work boots, get out the shovel, and start digging!

"Renovation Reflections"

1. What "wolves" threaten your recovery now?

2. What are you doing on a regular basis to build a solid foundation of recovery?

3. How are you becoming more like the little pig that opened his home to those in need?

Next: Appearances matter. Visualize a sober future that inspires confidence in others and pride in yourself.

Chapter 3

Curb Appeal

"I understood, through rehab, things about creating characters. I understood that creating whole people means knowing where we come from, how we can make a mistake and how we overcome things to make ourselves stronger."

~ Samuel L. Jackson

Imagine driving down a quiet street, looking for your dream home. What is it that's going to catch your eye and make you stop and think, "That's it! That's my new home. I can see myself living there." Your ideal home is one that is not only well suited for you on the inside, but you want one that has that "Wow" factor on the outside. It's what Realtors in the business refer to as "curb appeal."

You've got a good idea of what you want the exterior of your new abode to resemble. It needs to have certain characteristics. You know you want it to have some type of yard with neatly maintained hedges and flowers that bloom from early spring, throughout the summer and early into fall. No dead plants, overgrown weeds, or patchy grass for you.

In this imaginary world, your ideal home will also have a welcoming front porch, full of Southern charm. One that you can see yourself sitting on in a favorite rocking chair, with a sweet tea in your hand on a cool summer evening. (I did mention it was a porch with Southern charm, so of course, you'd be drinking sweet tea.) You'd be watching your neighbors as they pass by, walking their dogs, or looking at the children as they ride by on their bikes. Since this is your imagination, it goes without saying that the neighborhood you live in is going to have people that walk their dogs and children that still play outside rather than being hermetically sealed to their digital devices. This is your dream home, and you get to create the kind of neighbors that you want as well. You'll have hanging ferns and potted red geraniums on the porch. (Read - Southern porch again!)

Yes, your imaginary new home will have, without a doubt, charisma and curb appeal!

Ask any Realtor and they will tell you that genuine curb appeal is essential in real estate. Homes don't typically sell as well without. Why is it so important? First and foremost, it's the initial impression a potential buyer will have of a home. The exterior of the house and its surroundings are the first things that people see when they approach a house. Curb appeal provides a certain vibe that either appeals to the potential buyer, or not. This can be the determining factor as to whether the potential homeowner will pursue looking into the home. If the property doesn't "pop," the buyer may be less inclined to take a closer look, even if the interior of the home is impressive.

Curb appeal can shorten the time a home stays on the market. Not every person who is in the market to purchase a new home can see past an unkempt yard and overgrown gardens. Buyers are more likely to be attracted to a house that looks well-maintained. They often assume a well-maintained outside conveys the same existence inside the home.

What connection do curb appeal and recovery have in common, you may be asking yourself right now? At first glance, it may seem there is very little. In the rooms of 12 step meetings, we often talk about not comparing someone's outsides to our insides. However, as you think about what a life of addiction looks like life vs. a life in recovery, you begin to see the parallels between the two.

The visual of what that life really looks like can be the determining factor for someone to choose the path of recovery.

You see that curb appeal is the first impression a person has of their potential new home. When a person makes the decision to drop the drink or drugs and attempt to get clean and sober, the choice is often precipitated by a pause to look at what their life looks like to both them and those around them. It might be the first time that a person stops to examine the impact of addiction as it relates to their relationships, work, or their health. The visual of what that life really looks like can be the determining factor for someone to choose the path of recovery. Just as good curb appeal determines whether a potential buyer explores the possibility of pursuing the new home further, careful consideration of a life of continued consumption of substances that leads to unfortunate consequences can convince a person to choose recovery for a refurbished "exterior."

In addition, creating good curb appeal and getting sober typically require a significant amount of effort and unbridled commitment. Improving the curb appeal of a home may require the removal of dead plants and trees, pulling weeds that are choking out the beauty of overgrown flower beds, overseeding the yard to yield a plush carpet of green grass that beckons the owners to kick off their shoes and dig their bare feet into the luxurious lawn, replacing missing siding, or redoing an entire deck. Recovery may start with the hard road of detox, and it may involve weeding out people in your life that are detrimental to your sobriety, or you may find you need to remove yourself from certain environments that are now toxic to your sobriety. These endeavors require willingness to put in the work and bear the blisters that come with it to achieve the desired outcome.

The process of creating good curb appeal and embarking on the journey of sobriety share another important similarity: the sense of pride and beauty that emerges from the hard work invested. When I turn into the driveway of my own home and see the flower gardens that I have grown from seedlings and witness the beauty that abounds from it, it brings a sense of joy and delight to my heart. I recognize that so much of what is blooming, the colors that no crayon could accurately represent, did not all come to this beauty by my hands alone. I understand that I was responsible for deciding what seeds to plant, to research what might grow best in the spot that I had picked out given the amount of sun that could reach this garden spot. I dug the soil with the tools I had, planted the seeds, and was careful to mark the spot where I had planted them. I may have remembered to water them from time to time! Even without a green thumb, these plants somehow managed to grow.

Yet, in front of me now, is a rainbow of colors and a beautiful bouquet of fragrances that my nose tries desperately, without success, to identify.

I recognize that nature played a bigger role in the growth of the garden than I did. As the seed lay in its dormant state, the sun kissed the soil each morning, providing the warmth it needed to allow the seed to burst from its hull and to begin the process of creating roots. Roots are always the first part of the plant to grow. It anchors the plant much like the foundation of a house cements the home securely in place.

I recognize that nature played a bigger role in the growth of the garden than I did.

Nature also added her own plantings to the garden during its early stages. Unwelcome plants whose thought was to grow or perhaps even strangle out the plants I wanted to see bloom. WEEDS! But I was smarter than the weeds, recognizing them for what they were and the potential harm they would and could do if left to grow alongside my plants. I had worked too hard to provide the plants with all they needed to have the best chance of becoming the stunning beauties I knew they could be. The weeds had to go.

Our lives are so much like a garden, aren't they? Can you see times in your life when you have ever so carefully made plans? You search for the perfect spot in your life, the perfect time to start your project. You dig in the soil, adding the necessary nutrients to create the richest environment possible.

This plan you've created for yourself, if it's going to succeed, needs all the right things from the start. You plant. You water. You wait. Just as nature provides the elements necessary for growth and conversely, can also wreak havoc in our gardens, life doesn't always go as planned.

I live in the mountains of western North Carolina where frost and snow are often a part of the winter forecast. We expect to hear about the potential for frost in the winter months. Nature does not seem to follow the calendar. There are times when our apple trees are in full bloom in April, as is expected, and the weather will turn, hitting us with a biting frost–destroying the flowering buds, killing the possibility of new life, and crushing the heart and spirit of the farmer who depends on a bountiful crop. Perhaps you have experienced the bitter bite of the reality of the unexpected, much like the farmer.

The gardens of our life might be crowded with unwelcome weeds. How do we remove the weeds without destroying the plant, especially when it's in its infancy? It may require a special tool that allows the removal with the precision of a surgeon welding a scalpel. Pull out the weed without destroying the new growth. It's necessary to pull the weed out, root and all, or it will simply return.

If the garden is left unattended, growth does occur, however random it might be. Almost always though, the weeds win. I wonder why that is? Could it be that the weeds have been around so much longer? They are stronger. Their roots go deeper. The seeds we plant, it seems, are not as hardy as the weeds. They are more delicate and require more care. Yes, if left unattended, the weeds always win.

How then, do we ensure our garden grows the way we intended it to? The way we planned and hoped for? How do we grow a life that creates the beauty and sweet fragrance we desire? A garden with such abundance that it can easily be shared with others. Maybe we are careful about the type of plants we decide to plant in our life. What type of plants are you sowing for yourself? Anyone can plant a garden of flowers. But how you create it, what work you put in it will inevitably determine what eventually blooms.

 **"Renovation Reflections"**

1. What "weeds" continue to take over your garden of recovery?

2. What "seeds" would you like to plant and how will you cultivate the soil to ensure that they grow strong?

3. What are your greatest attributes that help your recovery grow?

Next: Set shame aside by making room in your life for relaxing and being yourself with people who care about you.

Chapter 4

Porch Sittin'

"The priority of any addict is to anesthetize the pain of living to ease the passage of day with some purchased relief."

~ Russell Brand

Prior to leaving the corporate world to pursue what I felt was my God-given purpose, I worked for a hospital system. I didn't work in direct patient care or in the hospital itself. I worked in the business development office just across the street from the hospital in a building that formerly housed a radiology practice. Working in an office building that had once been a medical building had its perks. One such perk was that it could only hold about 10 staff, so I worked with a small group of people. The other perk was that many of the offices had sinks in them! (For someone, like me, who is obsessive about teeth brushing, this is a huge perk!)

In this small hospital system, the business development office played a crucial role in supporting community outreach events sponsored by the hospital. Support was indeed provided! Our responsibilities ranged from hosting our own events to actively participating in events sponsored by the hospital or in collaboration with the local Chamber of Commerce.

Because we worked side by side on so many projects, we knew about each other's families and took a genuine interest in keeping up with what was going on in each other's lives. Conversations on Monday mornings after the weekend to catch up on what everyone did were a typical routine. Or we would spend a Friday afternoon finding out what plans each of us had for the upcoming weekend.

On one such occasion, I asked my neighboring officemate what she had planned for the weekend. She was relatively young and a native of this small rural community. She began to share her plans with me and said her two girlfriends were coming over to "do some porch sittin'."

"You're going to do what?" I asked in an extremely perplexed manner. I wasn't quite sure I'd heard her right because she had just used an expression I was completely unfamiliar with. Now, you need to know that I am from the South and yes, sometimes in the South, we use expressions that the rest of the country has never heard of. It's part of what makes being Southern so fun.

"Porch sittin'," she repeated and to my surprise that's exactly what I thought she said. My next question, of course, was what exactly is "porch sittin'"? Was it some type of Southern game I had never played?

She laughed and said it's simply sitting on the porch, drinking your beverage of choice, and catching up with everything that's been going on with each other. I had no idea this was even a thing, period. I'm not sure what other people call this or if there is even a term for it other than "porch sittin'" but I was intrigued. Why had I not heard of this sooner? I know people often just sit out on the front porch with friends but never knew it had a specific term. Now I know… and so do you, if you didn't.

Of course, I came home and asked Gary, who is also a native North Carolinian, about this new term I'd just been introduced to, and he too was familiar with this Southern slang. (He's also familiar with the term "skoshi bit" which I'd never heard of either, which means just a small amount of something.) Unfortunately, I have yet to find individuals to participate in this Southern tradition with me and I even have two oversized white wooden rockers on my front porch as well as a swing. I've certainly got all the makings of what must make porch sittin' successful.

I've certainly got all the makings of what must make porch sittin' successful.

I was feeling a bit sad that I was just now learning about this concept of porch sittin' at this stage in my life. How could I have not known? I lamented about all the fun and conversation I surely had missed out on over the years. I'm not sure if I've lived in homes that would have allowed for this leisurely activity. I began to consider all the homes in which I'd lived growing up, as well as homes in my adulthood.

As I began to reminisce about the past, my mind drifted to memories of my early childhood spent at my grandmother's. While my father was in the military and we moved almost every year for the first 10 years of my life, we always made our way to visit my grandparents for the holidays and for several weeks during the summer. As I thought about those special memories, a smile began to form on my face as images of sitting on their porch began to float in my mind. In that moment, I realized I had not, in fact, missed out on this simple Southern tradition. I had participated in it without being totally aware of it.

Some of my favorite memories of time spent at my grandparents' house were spent on a screened-in front porch. The relationship with grandparents is truly special and I am forever grateful for the precious times I was able to spend with "Mamaw" and "Papaw." (Now that's about as Southern as it gets, isn't it?) My parents often allowed my older sister and me to spend several weeks during the summer at my grandparents' house. We were given the freedom to ride horses, climb trees, play with dolls, and make mud pies to our hearts' delight, all while soaking in the lavish love of our grandparents. In retrospect, while we thought we were the lucky ones, I realize what a break it was for my parents to send not one, but both their children, to the grandparents' house for several weeks each summer! What most parents wouldn't give for that, right?

My grandparents had a farm, complete with large pastures that were home to several horses, a big red barn full of hay, a tack room that held all the riding gear, and feral cats that we tried desperately to tame that were there to keep the mice out of the grain. There was also a massive garden that would yield crops of corn, potatoes, peppers, tomatoes, cantaloupe, strawberries, peas, and bushels of green beans. We would help pick the beans and then begin the process of stringing and snapping them, readying them for the canning process.

Stringing beans on that porch was a summer tradition at my grandmother's house. It was semi-enclosed with windows all around. It held traditional 1950's metal outdoor furniture as well as several oversized rocking chairs. We'd have wooden baskets of beans in the middle of the red-tiled floor from which to gather a bunch to string and snap. I'd grab two handfuls of beans and put them onto the newspaper my grandmother had saved specifically for this purpose, that was laid out in front of me. Sitting cross-legged on the floor with a big stainless-steel pan in my lap ready to collect my work, I began the arduous task of stringing and snapping beans. (I still have that big pan and recall those special memories each time I use it.)

I wish I could recall the conversations that we had on that breezy, fan-cool porch on those lazy, hot summer afternoons but I remember those times fondly. I may not have always enjoyed stringing those beans, but I enjoyed the conversation and the time spent together. Those were good times spent with my grandmother, family, friends, and neighbors. I enjoyed "porch sittin'."

Perhaps porches are where we learn how to be friends with our neighbors. You can sit on your front porch and take in the street on which you live, or the neighborhood in which you reside. We are allowing others to see a glimpse of who we are without letting them fully into our lives. It's like taking a friendship for a test drive. We ask ourselves; do we want to know this person better or will they simply be "porch people" for us? It's a soft beginning and a good place to start.

When I was drinking, I didn't spend much time on my front porch. My presence on the front porch would expose what I was trying so desperately to hide. We get to know people on the front porch and decide whether we're going to let them in. It's safe on the front porch to explore friendships because we are only showing the external part of ourselves. Just like we are only showing the external part of our house. Some of us may ensure the outside looks good, that we have the right porch swing and pillows and flowers on the front porch, but inside our house can be somewhat of a disaster. The front porch can be very symbolic of our outward selves and who we share that part of ourselves with.

We get to know people on the front porch and decide whether we're going to let them in.

When you find yourself on the front porch in recovery, you begin to embrace your authentic self. It's a space where you can connect with the people who pass by. Stepping outside allows you to leave behind the shadows of isolation and engage with the vibrant tapestry of life unfolding in front of you. It is on the porch that you cultivate genuine connections, sharing stories, laughter, and support with those you allow to enter your home and your life. Opening the door and welcoming others signifies a willingness to let them see the vulnerable and imperfect part of your life. The part of you that no longer feels the need to hide.

Perhaps you've been hiding inside your home, secretly peering out the window as neighbors pass by, yearning to walk out onto the porch into the sunlight. In recovery, you can choose to step out on the porch, smell the fragrant flowers in the ceramic pots, and try out that porch swing. On the porch you can rediscover yourself, shedding the limitations of your past and embracing the possibilities of your newfound sobriety. Step out into the sunlight and savor it. Shed the cloak of shame and guilt. Cherish the connections forged there and embrace the beautiful renovation that is becoming your life.

Step out into the sunlight and savor it.

"Renovation Reflections"

1. If you're not stepping out onto your metaphorical front porch, what is keeping you from doing so?

2. What life lessons have you learned on the front porch that can serve you in your recovery?

3. Who are you in regular conversation with in your recovery journey?

Next: Every structure has a door. In recovery, it's essential to make deliberate choices about who is allowed entrance.

Chapter 5

Shut the Front Door

"I don't shut the door on it and I don't pretend it didn't happen."

~ Robert Downey, Jr.

If you've ever built a house or completed a renovation that involved replacing a front door, you may have experienced sticker shock when you start pricing this necessary part of your home. Who knew a door, the part of your house that lets people in or keeps people out, could be so expensive or come in such a wide variety of materials?

There are so many different styles of doors from which to choose. A local home improvement store will often carry the basic models designed to fit most homes. Higher end homes often require doors specially crafted to the specific dimensions of the opening. Exceptionally tall. Extra thick. Exotic material. All of these "extras" add to the character of the home and certainly to the bottom line of the price.

A dear friend once told me about an experience with a door that left a huge impression on me. She had moved from NC to California and was walking in her new neighborhood with a friend she had recently made. She had walked this route numerous times by herself and there was one house up on a hill that had the most ornate front door she had ever seen. It was so intricately designed and exceptionally big that it always caught her eye. She shared with me that secretly, she envied the door, the home, and the inhabitants. She imagined that if a home had such an incredible, gilded front door, the rest of the house would be just as spectacular. She envisioned the occupants had movie star looks, magnanimous personalities and lived a life she could only dream of. And yet, she willingly walked by this home regularly regardless of the envy in her heart.

But remember, if you want what's on the other side of that door, you must take everything that comes with it.

She'd never shared these thoughts of jealousy with her friend, but for some reason, this particular morning, on this particular walk, she confessed to her friend about the green-eyed monster that consumed her when she thought about what a wonderful life the family that lived behind those doors must have.

Her wise friend stopped her, put both hands on her shoulders, looked her directly in the eye, and gently said, "Yes, the door is beautiful. Remarkably so! I can understand that you think you want what's on the other side of that door. But remember, if you want what's on the other side of that door, you must take everything that comes with it. You may find it isn't as wonderful as you imagine."

"I know the family that lives in that house. The family behind that door," the wise friend continued with a glint of sadness spilling from her eyes. "The mother has terminal cancer, and the father lost his job a few months ago. They have one teenage son that is dealing with his own issues. So, while you see a beautiful door that seems to represent a beautiful life, the reality is much, much different."

She turned to my friend and asked her, "Now that you know the truth behind that door, would you still want it and all that comes with it?"

Oh, we are so quick to make judgments based on what we see. This is especially hard in the world of social media where people often show only the parts of their lives they want us to see, or a life they have curated to reflect what isn't actually there. We all know people who post on Facebook or Instagram with their picture-perfect kids and a spectacular spouse. What we don't see are the dozens of pictures they took and the filters they used to create the image they want others to believe is their reality.

I've never forgotten that story about the door. My friend is full of wisdom and I'm so grateful for all the things she shared with me. We could all use a friend like her.

Doors, like many other aspects of home building and renovations projects, must meet minimum safety and accessibility requirements. Did you know that any door that is used for an outside entrance must meet certain building codes? They must be able to withstand a certain degree of fire and come with a 'burn time' indicating how long it would take for the door to succumb to fire. Again, who knew? If you're like me, when you think about a front door, the two most important things to consider are what it looks like and how strong the locks are.

Part of my early adult life was spent in a city that was known for having a higher-than-normal crime rate. Mix that with someone who has a vivid imagination, and you get the makings of a horror movie script complete with a slasher and no escape. Strong, locked doors were very important to me.

Maybe the need to have all the doors in the house locked is because of the vivid memory I have of my dad ensuring the house was safe and secure before he went to bed. I can still picture him walking through the house, carefully checking each door to confirm it was locked. I don't remember him making a big deal out of it but for some reason, that ritual is embedded in my mind. I grew up thinking that's what every dad or spouse did. To my surprise, when I got remarried and Gary started off to bed without checking the doors, I was shocked! "Aren't you going to make sure all the doors are locked?" I questioned him as he continued to walk towards our bedroom. Clearly, I was going to have to explain to him that it was now his job. He looked at me perplexed, not completely understanding the issue. After I explained to him my childhood expectations, he willingly took on the role of "head door locker" at our home. We laugh about that conversation often and I've been known to lock the doors myself sometimes.

(I won't even address the conversation that took place when I learned that, prior to us getting married, he would often leave his own house unlocked. Needless to say, that does not occur in our house now. Never!)

As you might guess, with the imagination I've alluded to, having a grand front door with glass around the side of it or glass on any part of it was simply out of the question. It was easy to imagine someone breaking the glass, quietly slipping a black-gloved hand through the door and turning the knob to gain entrance into my home. Let's face it, we've all seen movies where that happens! No, doors need to be solid and strong. Doors were meant to keep unwanted visitors out!

What took me a long time to learn about doors was that they were also meant to let people in! When I was deep into my drinking, it was easy to justify not inviting people over to my house or into my life. No, I would keep the door closed to them. I hid behind the door both physically and emotionally. My best friend was always close by–in the form of a bottle of booze, a can of beer, or a carton of wine. Letting someone in meant exposing the reality of my life, one that I worked hard at keeping a secret.

Doors were meant to keep unwanted visitors out!

As contradictory as it may seem, while the door to my life was firmly held shut from the inside, so much of me longed to connect with what was on the other side of the door. On the other side, I would find out, was help and hope and eventually, sobriety. To achieve that, I had to find the courage to let down the facade of a perfect life. For a long time, no one outside the walls of my home knew I wrestled with the disease of alcoholism... and that I was consistently losing the match.

There is a common misconception regarding what an alcoholic or addict looks like. These stigmas and stereotypes can be harmful and potentially hamper someone from seeking the help they may need. There are many people whose first thought when they hear "alcoholic" or "addict" imagine someone experiencing homelessness, or a disheveled individual dressed in tattered clothing incapable of holding down a job. No one's mind envisions a well-suited, clean shaven or Christian Louboutin-shod individual with a six-figure income who shows up early to work every day. But the reality is that 70% of people struggling with a substance use disorder are employed either part time or full time.

Certainly, addictions can lead to unfortunate outcomes when left unchecked. Many individuals with a substance use disorder are considered high functioning because they have successful careers, intact families, and a thriving social life. Often, they've been able to hide their addiction while carefully orchestrating a facade of normalcy. It's important to understand that addiction is non-discriminating. It can affect anyone, regardless of gender, race, ethnicity, background, education, social, or religious status.

I remember a time at work, after I had returned from rehab, I shared with a co-worker where I had been for the past 30 days. (My employer was so gracious in allowing me the opportunity to go to a rehab for treatment and did not expose my "secret" to other employees.) When I shared this with my co-worker, I'll never forget what she said (which at my age, remembering what I had for breakfast is getting more difficult). She said, "Thank you for telling me that, Kit. I would never have guessed that you struggled with alcoholism. Your life looks so normal to others looking in."

It took me a few more years to be comfortable sharing my story, to open the door to a world that has so many misconceptions about alcoholism, addiction, and recovery.

Opening that door meant being vulnerable and required a willingness to step outside of my comfort zone. It meant exposing myself in a way that felt scary and freeing at the same time. What I didn't realize, in doing so, was that it allowed me to begin to connect with others in more meaningful ways.

I had learned that addiction thrives in the darkness of secrecy, but recovery blossoms in the light of transparency.

Doors can certainly let people in and it's important to remember that in recovery. In recovery, there are times in our lives when we also need to use doors to keep people out. We may find there are people we've allowed to have an all-access pass to our homes and our lives. We handed over the keys and allowed them to come and go at will. We may need to distance ourselves from individuals or situations that have the potential to trigger a relapse. The front door and the access it grants need to be monitored. We may need to close the door completely on unhealthy relationships as a means of self-care.

I had learned that addiction thrives in the darkness of secrecy, but recovery blossoms in the light of transparency.

In recovery, your front door should now require VIP designation and only those in your life that you choose to provide special backstage passes get to have access. Those that don't? Well, they can just get in line and wait like everyday folks! In early recovery, it can be hard to decide who gets access to the life you're trying to repair. The simplest question you can ask yourself about who to let in and who to keep out is will this person help or hinder your road to a renovated life of recovery.

"Renovation Reflections"

1. Who do you need to open the door of your life to, now?

2. Who do you need to start keeping out?

3. How are you gaining the skills to know the difference between who to let in and who to keep out?

Next: Recovery is about treating yourself well. And that includes choosing foods that are nourishing and wholesome.

Chapter 6

What's for Dinner?

"In recovery, I've realized the importance of creating a routine that supports my sobriety. It's about filling my days with activities that nourish my mind, body, and soul."

~ Ben Affleck

Heaven is going to be the place no one asks me, "What's for dinner?" Of that, I'm sure!

When my son, Tyler, was maybe around twelve or thirteen, he started the habit of coming into the kitchen when I was preparing dinner to see what I was cooking. He would stand over my shoulder, because at this point in his life he was as tall if not taller than I, examining whatever it was that I had simmering on the hot stove, or was mixing up in a bowl. We made every effort to sit at our kitchen table as a family most weeknights and eat a meal together. Even if we picked up a pizza on the way home from work, we ate together at the table. We even had a "no cell phones" tenet at the table! GASP! I know… it's a miracle no one called child protective services on me for inflicting and enforcing such a cruel rule!

He'd move from standing over my shoulder, to beside me. He'd lift the lid of a pot simmering on the stove or the lid of a crockpot and ask, "What time is dinner going to be ready?" He was a growing boy and food was of top priority. Well, food and girls! I'd give him a rough estimate of when it was going to be ready and then the following scenario played out almost nightly.

He'd go to the side-by-side refrigerator and open the door looking for something to snack on until dinner was ready. When nothing jumped out at him that might hold him over until dinner, he'd close the door and head to the pantry. There he'd open both doors, stand and stare at its contents and again, find nothing that would satisfy him. He'd swing the doors back and forth just a bit continuing to look and yet, still nothing. So, he'd close (read SLAM) the doors and go back to the fridge. With a firm grip on the cool handles of the fridge, he'd slowly reopen. It was as if he envisioned a flight of whimsical food fairies magically filling it with morsels that would satiate his hunger, or perhaps they had rearranged the contents, unveiling food that had somehow eluded his initial inspection. Still nothing. Repeat pantry inspection. Ask again, "What time is dinner?" Open fridge. Close fridge. Open pantry. Close pantry. Sigh! If you've ever had a pre-teen boy, you know exactly what I'm talking about. It might even include some type of eyeroll. He'd resign himself to the fact that supper would have to suffice.

Ah, the sacred ritual of foraging the fridge and pantry in search of sustenance. It's a dance all of us know all too well! If we're honest, we've all indulged in this activity countless times ourselves. (If I could insert an emoji here, it would be the one with a raised hand.) Gary will witness my back-and-forth performance between the pantry and the refrigerator and say, "Do you think something that you want is just going to magically appear if you keep doing that enough?" Of course, I know it isn't, and yet, I repeat that same pattern, always yielding the same result.

While that memory of my son's incessant food sourcing is still a memory I cherish, it's tainted by the fact that in addition to fueling my family with food while I was cooking, I was feeding my addiction to alcohol. I usually started drinking as soon as I got home from work. Start dinner, start drinking. I kept a jelly jar filled with white wine beside the stove most nights while I cooked and would take big gulps while my son glared into the fridge. (Why I chose a jelly jar, I have no idea.) Wine was rarely used for cooking–it was mainly for consumption.

I learned a new definition of insanity when I started going to AA. I was told "Insanity is doing the same thing over and over again expecting different results." I'm sure that definition has been used outside the walls of 12 step meetings. It certainly is a concept any of us can relate to, right? Haven't we all stood in front of the proverbial empty fridge or pantry of life, hoping for a miraculous replenishment?

Wine was rarely used for cooking – it was mainly used for consumption.

That seems to be human nature: wanting a different outcome but continuing to choose behaviors that don't move the needle in the right direction. What doors in your life do you continue to open only to find the same contents? How many times do we repeat unhealthy patterns in our lives that continue to yield the same, if not worse, results?

We choose to scarf down unhealthy foods and eventually discover those choices created chronic diseases such as high blood pressure or type 2 diabetes. We opt for excess calories instead of expending them and yet we feel betrayed by elevated numbers on the bathroom scale when we step on them. I recently heard a quote that appears to be attributed to Zig Ziglar that resonates with me: "Don't be upset by the results you didn't get by the effort you didn't give."

We choose a sedentary lifestyle. It's easier to take the elevator than the stairs. It feels better to stay up late binging on the latest Netflix series than to go to bed at a reasonable hour so we can get up 30 minutes early to exercise. We'd rather meet our friends for lunch at our favorite restaurant than to lace up our tennis shoes and walk a few laps around the local park.

We choose to spend more than we make. When we see a spectacular sale on a special seasonal sweater while our bank statement is void of the proper funds to afford it, it's easy to pull out the credit card and charge it. We want a luxury car, but our finances only allow for a budget vehicle. We regularly run out of money before we run out of month.

I'm not sure if those who experience a substance use disorder or addictive behavior can pinpoint when or where it started. There are so many reasons people find themselves bogged down by behaviors that are not conducive to the life they'd like to be living. I believe I can say with almost all certainty that no child, when asked what they want to be when they grow up, ever responds with, "I dream of becoming an alcoholic" or "I want nothing more than to be addicted to drugs."

The kitchen was once one of the battlegrounds where addiction waged war in my life and it has also become a site of victory in recovery. It's ironic that one of the very places I fueled my disease has become a source of salvation. Exercise was a big part of my recovery, so it stands to reason that creating healthy eating habits was equally important.

I also learned how easy it could be to trade one addiction for another–especially when it comes to food, particularly sugar. Over the past few years, there has been increasing research on the similarities between addiction to alcohol and sugar. The latest medical research suggests that sugar addiction may be as real and serious as alcohol addiction, as both substances trigger similar responses in the brain and the body.

When we consume sugar, the bacteria in our gut can become imbalanced, leading to an overgrowth of harmful bacteria. This can cause inflammation, which can affect the brain's reward centers, leading to cravings for more sugar. In fact, some studies have found that sugar can be as addictive as drugs like cocaine, activating similar areas of the brain.

Another way that sugar addiction is like alcohol addiction is that both substances can lead to a cycle of cravings and withdrawal. When we consume sugar, our body releases dopamine, a neurotransmitter that makes us feel good. However, over time, our brain becomes desensitized to dopamine, leading to a need for more sugar to achieve the same pleasurable effects. When we try to cut back on sugar, we may experience withdrawal symptoms, such as headaches, irritability, and cravings. I can tell you from personal experience, the cravings associated with sugar are similar to the cravings for alcohol.

It's difficult for people who have never struggled with addictions to truly understand the challenges faced by those who do. They might view it as a simple matter of willpower or self-control. Oh, if it were just that simple! Addiction is a complex disease that affects not only the body but also the mind and spirit. Fortunately, the kitchen of recovery provides restoration to all three. It's a place where you learn how to nourish your body and mind in a way that supports your sobriety journey. A restored mind and body allow for a refurbished soul. Cooking and eating healthy foods become an essential part of your recovery process. At its core, the kitchen of recovery is a place of community. It's a space where you can gather and share your stories, your struggles, and your triumphs with your invited guests.

> *Addiction is a complex disease that affects not only the body but also the mind and spirit.*

For me, alcohol was not just a drink to be enjoyed. It was my comfort and escape from the stress and pain of everyday life. It was my crutch, my support system, my best friend, and my worst enemy. Addiction is a chronic disease that requires ongoing attention. It's a battle that is fought every day, and even the smallest slip-up can lead to a relapse.

When a coaching client tells me they're ready to stop drinking, want to lose weight, or make an important career change, one of the first questions I ask is, "What makes this important to you now?" It helps them determine their "why", which is what they will need to come back to repeatedly when it starts getting hard to stay on track. That's a good question to ask yourself in early recovery and to continue to ask yourself. Your reasons may change, but it's so important to have a reason you can recall when your recovery is in jeopardy.

Fortunately, the years in sobriety have provided the opportunity to rewrite some of those stories. The kitchen is the heart of our home, the place where we gather to prepare and share meals. It is a space where precious new memories around mealtime have been made, where stories have been shared, and where love is poured into every dish. And sometimes, even now when my son comes home for a visit, he still repeats the refrigerator/pantry repertoire... and I just smile.

 **"Renovation Reflections"**

1. What's your "why" for wanting to start or stay in recovery?

2. What unhealthy patterns do you need to change to ensure you stay on a solid path of recovery?

3. Have you traded one unhealthy addiction for another? If so, what and when are you going to do something about it?

Next: It can take more than a new coat of paint to remodel the close relationships and ingrained practices that supported your addiction.

Chapter 7

Family Room

"In the darkest times, my family's unwavering faith in me kept me going and helped me overcome my addiction."

~ Robert Downey, Jr.

When I first began to make small changes to some of my previous homes, I was often, if not always, somewhat intoxicated. If I wasn't inebriated at the beginning of the project, you could bet I would be by the time I was finished. I would judge the size of the project based on the number of beers I thought I could consume from start to finish. You know, a project that takes a couple of hours would be a six-pack project. An evening project was typically a 12-pack project, and an all-day yard project was one in which I could potentially consume a whole case. I'll never forget the first time I painted a room sober! As it turns out, I was a much better painter sober! Imagine that! Painting while I was drinking was like an adult version of coloring inside the lines, except the lines were not always straight and sometimes the colors didn't match.

Thank goodness I didn't graduate to the larger projects I've undertaken until I entered recovery. Mixing a miter saw with a Moscow Mojito might not have been the best combination.

The family room serves as a common gathering spot for cherished ones and is frequently among the initial areas that receive a makeover when a new homeowner takes charge. Typically, this is where the television is located, so it's the place where people congregate after a long day at work, or once homework has been completed. Isn't it ironic that we consider family time, time that we are simply in the same room with each other, yet our eyes and ears are transfixed on an inanimate object projecting images meant to entertain us? There's really no interaction and if someone dares to talk during the show, they are quickly reprimanded with a loud "Shhh!" by the other occupants. No wonder we think the family room is the place you go to unwind and relax, until the rest of your family discovers you there and ruins it for you!

As a potential home buyer, the location of the family room, the size of it and how it's configured, can be the determining factor in whether or not to purchase the home. If it has the right dimensions but is lacking in other aesthetically pleasing properties, the home buyer might decide there are some minor renovations that will create a room that allows the chaos of a family to be organized into a cozy mess. Alas, awaken the DIY'er!

Painting a room is a marvelous way to transform a mundane space into a magical masterpiece. Picking the perfect paint pigment practically requires a degree in fine art as the color of that small sample you select in the store is almost never the same once it's slathered on the wall. Somehow, the lighting in a room, whether natural or artificial, can dramatically impact the exact hue that comes through.

Sobriety can be a lot like that as well. What we envision it to be like when we see just a tiny snapshot of it reflected in someone else's life is probably not what it's going to look like in your own. It may take a couple of trips to the home improvement store and good old fashion trial and error before you find just the right shade that brings out the very best in the room. You must find the color of sobriety that looks the best on you.

Tackling a family room renovation may seem like a daunting task. As you stand amid the four walls of this room, you may find that they are absent of any color, the floors are covered with outdated and worn carpet, and the furniture is not at all to your liking. At first glance, it's hard to imagine how this room, that feels in such disarray in this current moment, can be rejuvenated into a relaxing and welcoming space. Similarly, when you first consider embarking on a life of recovery, it can feel overwhelming. You may have no idea where to begin and what steps to take first. You may be feeling that way even now.

You must find the color of sobriety that looks the best on you.

It's ok to feel overwhelmed. After all, you're addressing the room that is used by every member of the family. In recovery, rebuilding family relationships that have been neglected or abandoned, can feel staggering. Part of the process of renovating a room often starts by clearing out the clutter. It makes it a heck of a lot easier to work in a room that is devoid of unneeded items. Sometimes part of the declutter process includes making minor repairs such as patching small holes in the walls prior to applying a fresh coat of paint, removing any outdated furniture, or taking down window treatments that are old and out of style. Similarly, repairing relationships might begin with small steps like breaking bad habits or learning to effectively communicate by listening to how your actions have affected others.

Of course, almost anyone who has ever painted a room as a mini makeover begins to find other aspects of the room that need attention. The furniture that once seemed so well-suited no longer creates the ambience the freshly painted walls provide. The curtains that once covered windows are no longer wanted as newly selected paint pops when the sun's morning rays filter through the glass of tall windows. The color of the carpeted floor seems to clash with the newly painted walls and would look so much better if it were hardwood. If hardwood isn't an option, at least a new area rug might do the trick. Yes, the one small project of painting quickly snowballs into a multi-faceted makeover.

So it is in sobriety. Initially, you're just focused on not drinking or using, one day at a time. But as the sober days turn into sober weeks and months, and the walls of sobriety start to take shape, other life issues are revealed and demand attention. You find there are people, places, and things that once seemed suitable and now no longer fit the ambiance of your newly sober life. Old habits and routines that once covered up the pain and difficulties of addiction are no longer necessary and are discarded. Just as newly painted walls demand new pictures, the clarity of a sober life highlights the need for healthy relationships, positive activities, and fulfilling goals. The carpet of a life once cluttered with addiction can be replaced with the hardwood of resilience and strength. A new rug of self-care and self-love added as a beautiful accent. The single act of getting sober can lead to a multi-faceted makeover of life, revealing a more authentic and content version of oneself.

Adding light to a life that has been lived in the darkness takes time.

One of the most rewarding aspects of any renovation is seeing progress. The old made new. Sometimes it seems like a slow process, much like recovery. Adding light to a life that has been lived in darkness takes time. It's like walking out in the light of a brilliant day and needing a few minutes for your eyes to adjust to the magnitude of the sun's light. It can also be easy to get discouraged when progress slows or sometimes even feels like there's a setback, or unexpected challenge, but perseverance makes anything possible.

As the major renovations of the family room wind down, the opportunity to add the personal touches to the room that make it yours begins. This is when it gets fun! Hanging pictures that reflect your personality, adding colorful throw pillows to the couch along with a cozy blanket to snuggle up in, or added tchotchkes that may only have meaning to you. All these little touches make the room feel like home, like healing, like you.

Shortly after I admitted to my employer that I was struggling with an active addiction to alcohol and decided I needed to go rehab, she and her husband came to my house to talk with Gary and me. They had walked in our footsteps with the roles reversed. She was the one who had endured the heartache and frustration that came with being married to an alcoholic. It was also the first time Gary had ever openly talked about not only my addiction but the impact it had on him. I will be forever grateful for the opportunity Gary had to fully express his feelings. For once in my life, I just listened. I heard the hurt.

As you continue to make changes to your family room, it may require you to think outside the box to find solutions to unforeseen challenges. You may have a smaller living space and need to find creative ways to maximize storage and seating. Similarly, overcoming addiction may necessitate finding creative ways to deal with new stresses and old triggers. Renovating a family room and creating a new life from addiction both require hard work, patience, and determination. It's not always easy, but the result is worth it. As the room takes shape and your new life begins to emerge, you'll feel a sense of pride and accomplishment.

The beauty of a remodeled life is that sometimes all it takes are a few minor changes to create a warmth and glow that become so incredibly inviting. A once hardened heart comes to life when the flames of joy are fed with the kindling of kindness and gratitude. The eyes that once seemed so empty begin to reflect love and light as the scales of shame begin to shrivel and fall away. A soul that seemed lost finds a new sense of purpose and direction as old patterns and limiting beliefs are released and painted with a fresh coat of perspectives and a refurbished sense of hope. Each day is a new opportunity to embrace the beauty of the present moment and to create a brighter future.

So, as you pick up that hammer to nail down your future, or a jar of spackling to repair the holes in your relationships, remember that progress takes time and effort. Take heart, and trust in the power of change, for a remodeled life is always within reach, waiting to be discovered, embraced, and lived to the fullest.

"Renovation Reflections"

1. What relationships in your life of recovery need a makeover?

2. What are you consistently doing to discover what your new sober life needs?

3. What fun activities or habits have you added to your renovated recovery?

Next: The dining room should be a place to share abundance and love with people we care about–not a formal place full of rules, fear, and judgment.

Chapter 8

Dining Room Diva

"Ya think that the whiskey tastes good? Try a big cup of sobriety – now that is the good stuff!"

~ Steven Tyler

What ever happened to formal dining rooms? Is it just me, or does it seem like not many new homes have true dining rooms as part of the floor plan? Open-floor plan. That's what most people want. Everything open. The dining room, kitchen and living room/family room flow together–no walls separating them. Never really being sure where one room stops and the other begins.

There are advantages to an open floor plan, especially for young families. It's easy to keep an eye on young children to ensure they aren't painting the floor with crayons or eating them while parents are puttering around in the kitchen. The ability to socialize and communicate with family members is made easier without walls. (True both literally and figuratively, right?) Personally, I like an open floor plan but there are some drawbacks that I experience, and I wonder if you might as well. Like, when you're watching TV in the living room, and someone turns on the water in the sink in the kitchen. At my age, I can't hear the TV over the water running.

What I discovered about open floor plans, as I did a little research for this writing, was that they began to make their way into the architectural world in the 1950s when entertaining in the home became less formal. Prior to this, the kitchen was typically located at the back of the house and a formal living room or dining room was in the front of the home. A long hallway allowed access to bedrooms. By the 1990s, an open floor plan was pretty much the norm for most new builds. Of course, now we know that almost everyone winds up in the kitchen during a gathering. Still haven't quite figured that out yet!

As children, we all have dreams of what we want our grown-up world to look like. We create certain milestones that mark our desired accomplishments, like getting our driver's license, being able to vote, graduating from high school or college, or getting our first job. Maybe, even now, you're still working towards some of yours. Maybe achieving sobriety is the biggest milestone in your life so far. If so, it's a huge accomplishment and one to be exceptionally proud of!

Maybe achieving sobriety is the biggest milestone in your life so far.

I was in my early 30s when I thought I had surely arrived! It wasn't a milestone I had set for myself, but nonetheless one that felt monumental. I found myself in my newly purchased home that was not only located in the local country club, but we had also been able to join the club as members. It's funny how we decide what constitutes "arriving" in our lives. Being a member of the country club was probably more my ex-husband's idea of arriving than mine. He was a golfer and certainly utilized the membership for that purpose, but we could enjoy the summer activities it offered. My son enjoyed the Olympic size pool while I enjoyed the beer service I had access to. Living within walking distance of the pool had its advantages. It meant I could drink without the worry of having to drive home–something I still thought about at that point in my drinking.

Behind the closed doors of my home, my world was dark.

At the age of 33, by the world's standards, I was living a perfect life. I was married and a stay-at-home mom of a precious little boy. I lived in a lovely home, had a vacation condo at the beach, attended a church filled with numerous prominent members of the community, and had my house professionally cleaned weekly and my yard mowed regularly. Behind the closed doors of my home, my world was dark, and I was living a lie. All these symbols of prestige did nothing for the ache in my soul. I still felt like I wasn't enough. That feeling of not being enough, I would eventually discover, contributed greatly to my excessive drinking.

I remember another specific milestone moment that felt like I had arrived at the place I wanted to be in life, when I paid $50 for a Christmas sweater! I had never paid that much for a sweater! That was in the mid 90s… and I still have that sweater! I don't ever wear it, but I'll never forget the thrill it gave me to purchase it. Of course, it didn't change how I felt about myself overall but there was something about purchasing it that made me feel good. I suppose I could have just as easily become a shopaholic in addition to being an alcoholic. Anything that numbed the swirling feelings of insecurity that plagued me daily would be a welcome alternative to sitting with those feelings. Shopping, food, alcohol, drugs... they can all be forms of self-medicating behaviors that eventually, if misused, become harmful rather than helpful, and certainly a long way from healing. (When my first husband and I divorced and I began to pack my belongings to move to a new location, I was surprised at the clothes hanging in my closet with the tags still on them. Yes, retail therapy was another way I dealt with the emptiness in my heart.)

As a young wife to my first husband, I recall having a small dinner party at our new home in the country club. For the first time in our married life, we had a formal dining room. With great care and attention to detail, I meticulously furnished the room with a classic cherry dining room table set, complete with matching chairs. To add a touch of elegance, I invested in host and hostess chairs, carefully placed at both ends of the table. I even remember choosing wallpaper that would coordinate with the fine china I would use when hosting dinner parties. (Wallpaper was all the rage at that time!) The invited guests at this particular dinner party were mostly my husband's friends, not mine. I felt the need to impress them because I believed their social status was important for my own life. As a young woman struggling with insecurity and lacking self-confidence, I had misplaced priorities. I've come to understand that true wealth lies not in material possessions, but in the richness of

I've come to understand that true wealth lies not in material possession, but in the richness of character.

character. With sobriety and maturity, my skewed priorities gave way to a stronger sense of self and serenity.

Perhaps it was the feelings of insecurity, of not being enough, that were raised when one of the women at the dinner party I had so carefully put together, picked up her plate at her place setting, turned it over to look at the maker of it. I remember sitting there, at my dining room table, set with the best china I owned and recently polished silverware, thinking *Who does she think she is? Is she looking at the china to determine whether it's good enough for her to eat from?* I was so indignant at her curiosity. I immediately processed it through the filter of insecurity, concluding that I must not be good enough, or that my china was not good enough…. Nothing was ever good enough. I carried that feeling with me into every situation and drank in an effort to escape it. Of course, you never escape it… drinking is merely a temporary salve for wounds that run deep, with their beginnings rooted in negative life experiences long ago.

Looking back now, so many years later and with a filter of healing, of restoration, I interpret that scenario a little differently. Rather than immediately choosing to believe my guest was looking at the plate to see if it was suitable for her high-class liking, she may have noticed the delicate pattern on the plate and simply wanted to know who made this elegant china. The small pink roses, the dainty green petals, and the gold etching on the outer ring of the plate were exquisite. The china had been my mother's, given to her by her mother-in-law. Even if the pattern wasn't beautiful, which it was, it certainly held sentimental value. And that should have been enough. I was enough then. I am enough now.

In a room meant for formality, we can find ourselves feeling fearful. Fearful of being exposed as a fraud. That incident occurred literally decades ago, and I still so vividly picture that plate being turned over in the hands of someone I thought I needed to matter to. That woman who sat at my table, on that evening, has probably never thought of that moment or me, since then!

Addictions can occur for a multitude of reasons. I think a huge part of my addiction resulted from my inability to view myself with acceptance and love. Alcohol was my drug of choice and I used it to desperately try to escape my feelings of insecurity and low self-esteem. In an intoxicated state, the pain was dulled for a while; it was tolerable even though the numbing effect was only temporary.

For some of us, it may be impossible to pinpoint where our insecurities come from. Negative experiences of loss and separation, especially at a young age, can lodge a wedge in our ability to view our current circumstances accurately. Abuse, neglect, rejection, and criticism from others can be perceived as evidence that we are not deserving of being cared for and loved, and internalized as not being good enough.

Once we've developed these deep-seated feelings of self-doubt about who we are, it can be difficult to change them or turn them around. They may lead to feelings of depression and anxiety which can propel us down a path of compulsive behavior that is often self-destructive. Almost without knowing it, alcohol, drugs, sex, or other substances can become a way in which we believe we can manage these feelings. Suddenly, the fear subsides, and we feel as if we are 10 feet tall and bullet-proof. Unfortunately, these substances may ease the pain, but they don't heal the wound of insecurity.

What then, are we to do with these emotions of fear and insecurity? How did they contribute to our addiction? As we take our place at the table of recovery and begin to enjoy each course as it's served, savoring each delectable dish, we recognize the abundance right in front of us. We see our journey is full of goodness. We recognize those seated at the table with us are there to support us without judgment. After all, at this point in our recovery, these are the guests we invited to join us.

 **"Renovation Reflections"**

1. What situations in your life might need to be revisited through the lens of recovery?

2. What new milestones have you set for yourself in recovery?

3. How are you learning to let go of limiting beliefs about yourself to allow you to move forward with confidence?

Next: Recovery is hard work. Your load is lightened by people who support you and small daily tasks to build your sense of self-worth with frequent victories.

Chapter 9

Productivity and Pajama Pants

"In recovery, I've discovered the importance of creating healthy habits to protect my sobriety. It's about prioritizing self-care and making choices that align with my values and goals."

~ Kelly Osbourne

WFH. Not to be confused with WTF. Although WTF was probably what countless people thought when the idea of WFH became the norm in the spring of 2020 when COVID penetrated our workforce and world. In case you're like me and still somewhat befuddled by all the social media acronyms… WFH is "work from home" and well, WTF is "What the F*%k." I'm guessing not all of you holding this book in your hands have uttered those words when faced with an incredibly baffling situation, but honestly, 2020 would have been the year you may have at least thought about it! I still SMH when I think about it. (Read "shake my head.")

Ok, I'll stop! The idea of working from home became a normal necessity for so many people to continue their employment during the years we dealt with COVID. How parents with young or school age children ever managed to juggle their own work, their children's virtual school and all the other issues facing them during that time still amazes me!

Of course, there were all the essential workers unable to work from home. They became our heroes. In those early months of the pandemic, we hailed our first responders and front-line hospital personnel for their willingness to put their lives on the line. Day in and day out, they worked tirelessly to try to save those individuals that had contracted COVID19. The news reported how some health care providers were sleeping at the hospital and not going home to keep their precious family safe. When they mustered the courage to return home, we heard how they shed the garments worn during their time at the hospital right outside their residences, even in harsh weather conditions like freezing temperatures or heavy rainfall. They stuffed the clothing in a bag, intending to have it thoroughly disinfected in the wash. They quickly made their way indoors, seeking the solace of a shower, desperately hoping to cleanse every conceivable trace of the virus that might linger upon their bodies.

My husband was considered an essential worker since he worked for UPS. I guess you could say he had a mobile office. In the early months of the pandemic, some of his customers asked him to leave their packages at the door so they could spray or wipe them down with sanitizer before bringing them into their homes. A few cautious recipients decided to delay bringing the parcels indoors for several days, ensuring they were free from any potential traces of the virus.

In the first couple of weeks of the pandemic, I made my husband take off his shoes before coming in the house and go straight to the laundry room to remove his uniform. We wiped doorknobs, sprayed disinfectant, and practically soaked our hands with sanitizers. We still knew very little about the virus and what we did know was that many people were dying because of it. It was a scary time.

During this time, we elevated our essential workers and gave them a new sense of worth. We celebrated the grocery store workers and delivery drivers. We had "healthcare heroes" and "front-line champions" who were brave and selfless–making tremendous sacrifices in the face of this horrific virus. Everywhere you looked, from TV, to social media posts, to billboards, we saw praise and thanks to this incredible group of people who were, even in the face of death, willing to continue their work. They were like the Avengers of the real world, bravely battling the invisible villain that had suddenly taken over our lives. (Remember the tagline, "Not all heroes wear capes; some wear scrubs"?) We showed our appreciation for them by cheering as they entered the hospitals, thanking them when we went through the line at the grocery store, and even leaving gifts for our delivery drivers on our porches.

A normal where worth was placed on essential service not lavish luxury.

These hard-working heroes were keeping us fed, picking up our trash, providing life-saving medicine, preparing our food, and keeping us safe. Yes, these essential workers were crucial!

What the world valued changed during the first part of the pandemic. We were grateful to the grocery stores for keeping their doors open and thankful for the restaurants that figured out a way to allow us to get take-out or utilize delivery services. Slowly, we created a new normal for this moment in time. A normal where worth was placed on essential service not lavish luxury. Hollywood seemed silenced (I mean, you couldn't go to the movies!) and everyday workers were elevated!

We bestowed upon these workers a renewed sense of significance, acknowledging, and appreciating the invaluable contributions they had been making all along. Almost as swiftly as we elevated them to this newfound importance for their genuinely essential work, it appeared that our collective memory faded as the pandemic subsided. Not only did we remove their metaphorical "capes," but for many, we unintentionally undermined their sense of self-worth. Their actions remained unchanged; what altered was our perception of their work and its profound impact on our daily existence.

What makes having self-worth so important? Without it, it's possible you may lean towards having negative self-talk and doubt. You may struggle to set healthy boundaries for yourself in your relationships. A high sense of self-worth helps you set and pursue goals that push you outside of your comfort zone, while allowing you to feel a sense of achievement when you attain or surpass them. Ultimately, self-worth is about knowing your own inherent value as a human being, regardless of external factors like successes, possessions, or social status. It's a great trait to possess and not always an easy one to grasp.

For anyone who has ever struggled with self-worth, I get it. I wonder if it's one of the reasons we chose to medicate ourselves with our substance of choice. To numb that sometimes dull, sometimes deafening cry of feeling "less than." The alcoholic pours liquid courage down their throat hoping to tighten the loose screws of self-esteem. The addict seeks to squelch the screams in their head, a cacophony of torment and turmoil. The person suffering with bulimia or anorexia purges food as if it were an eraser, trying to wipe away their perceived flaws and mistakes, or the person who struggles with food addictions tries desperately to stuff their shameful feelings with food. But all the while, numbing is only possible for a few moments.

We allow what others think to determine our self-worth.

I've struggled with these feelings of low self-worth most of my life. Perhaps you have as well. We allow the world to determine how we are to define worth and so much of it depends on the letters that follow our name on our business cards, or the number of zeros we see in our annual salary. Do we own expensive homes, drive luxury cars, vacation in exotic places, or wear clothes whose labels read Louis Vuitton, Gucci, or Hermes? Although these are all external factors, many of us allow them to define who we are internally. We allow what others think to determine our self-worth.

For many people in recovery, renovating your self-worth can be a considerably challenging and ongoing battle with the committee that meets frequently in your head that concludes you are not, in fact, enough. Regaining and rebuilding your self-worth in recovery becomes vitally important for maintaining sobriety and allowing you the opportunity to create a new and improved self-image: A refurbished version of you. As you begin to celebrate and honor your sobriety and give it a sacred place in your life, you begin to see it as an incredibly significant event. It becomes a major milestone.

As I work with employers seeking the designation as a "recovery friendly workplace," I often share parts of my personal journey towards recovery. It was a pivotal moment when my employer supported me in attending rehab. Just picture the liberation felt by someone in recovery when they're asked in an interview, "What's your greatest achievement?" and they can answer honestly. Without the fear of judgment, they can proudly say, "Overcoming addiction and achieving sobriety is one of my greatest accomplishments." As the fear of stigma declines, we're finding freedom in proudly proclaiming our recovery successes. The depths of our struggles often reflect the heights of our potential.

Building back a better self-worth begins with self-compassion. Learn to be kind to yourself; you are worthy of love and respect. Celebrate the small successes in sobriety. Setting small, realistic goals is a great way to rebuild your self-worth. Surround yourself with people who support and encourage your new lifestyle. Let others love you until you can love yourself.

Remember that creating self-worth is a process that takes time and effort. Be patient with yourself as you continue to work on building a positive self-image. Self-worth is not a destination to reach, but a journey to embrace. It is one of the building blocks to living a fulfilling and authentic life. Believe and accept that you are enough, just as you are.

 **"Renovation Reflections"**

1. What gives you a sense of self-worth now?

2. How have your priorities changed in recovery?

3. How are you embracing recovery as a significant accomplishment in your life?

Next: Your recovery structure isn't complete without a place you can spend time alone as you practice prayer, meditation, mindfulness, or whatever it takes to build up your strength.

Chapter 10

Sweet Retreat

*"But addiction wakes up before you do, and it wants you
alone. Alcoholism will win every time."*

~ Matthew Perry,
Friends, Lovers, and the Big Terrible Thing

A friend told me about a conversation she had with her coworkers regarding her recent bedroom remodel. While she saw the ongoing disarray as a disaster, her younger colleagues found it intriguing. One of them even said, "That sounds like so much fun! It must be like camping... but indoors!" To them, the idea of sleeping on the floor and eating takeout every night in a house with heat and running water resembled "glamping." My friend, on the other hand, strongly disagreed and said, "I can assure you; it doesn't feel like glamping to me. It feels like one big mess!"

The house my friend and her husband lived in was built by a builder who intended it to be his personal residence. The bedrooms were on the smaller side, which was a common feature in new homes built in the late 2000s. The focus was more on spacious kitchens that seamlessly connected to the family room, creating a smooth flow for entertaining. This design concept was highly sought after by many homebuyers. However, in practice, its effectiveness varied. The builder and his wife, for instance, had chosen to have separate bedrooms due to one of them being an exceptionally loud snorer. I'll leave it to your imagination to figure out which one!

To improve the chances of selling their house at a higher price, the couple decided to make the bedroom and the connected bathroom larger. This would create a special and luxurious space known as the "owner's retreat." It's fascinating how we now refer to the biggest bedroom in a home as a place for the owner to retreat. I wonder how many people truly consider their bedroom as a sanctuary, or if they have any sacred space in their home at all. My friend also mentioned that once you start one renovation project, it makes sense to add smaller renovations, too. It's just more convenient to do them all together, isn't it?

Adding to the bedroom/bathroom renovation included pulling up the carpet in the other two bedrooms and hallway to install hardwood floors that would match the new hardwood floors in the bedroom. They also assured us this renovation was being done solely for the purpose of making the room more suitable to their lifestyle–they did sleep in the same bed and wanted a room that would accommodate a king-size bed. Not sure if either of them snored!

As a result, their living room became their temporary living space, filled with chaos. Mattresses were squeezed between the couch and loveseat, dressers lined the walls, and clothes that were usually neatly hung in the closets now covered the dining room table. The piles of clothes were still on hangers. The contractor estimated that everything would be finished by the second or third week of January. However, she'd shared this news with me during the first week of December. "Why now?", I thought to myself, questioning the decision to start such a major project that caused so much disruption during an already busy time of the year. Nonetheless, I kept my thoughts to myself, unable to fathom willingly undertaking such a significant endeavor during the holiday season. My friend explained, "This was the only time the contractor could do it, so we had to choose between now or an uncertain future."

Every home should have a designated space where one can find peace.

Do it now or wonder when it will get done. I'm sure there are many people who apply that philosophy to their lives. Those are the people who, unlike me, and maybe you as well, don't practice the powerful art of procrastination. I've spent so much of my life perfecting it. I had to admire her willingness to dive headfirst into such a huge project during an already stressful season. Kudos to her.

I understand her longing to create a personal sanctuary, a place where she could retreat. Every home should have a designated space where one can find peace. I wonder if you have found yours? For me, the closet served as my asylum during my drinking days. It was where I concealed my bottles, and I would sneak there to take a few substantial swigs while preparing dinner or during TV commercials after dinner. (I didn't start hiding my drinking until I attempted to quit and realized I couldn't. Instead of admitting the challenges I faced,

I resorted to lying. I told my husband I wasn't drinking, and for the longest time, he believed me.)

We joke about men having their "man cave" room and women desiring to have a "she shed" and of course, almost every child would like to have a playhouse or a tree fort. It seems to be an innate desire to have a place we can call our own–even from a young age. A place that provides a sense of retreat. Perhaps that is how the largest bedroom in the home garnered the title of "owner's retreat."

When we bought the house in which we currently live, I wanted to make a spot in the house that would be my personal "retreat." It would be the place for my quiet time, to reflect on the day as I penned pages of my journal, or the place I could start my day in devotion and prayer, thankful for the many blessings I have been given–sobriety being one of the best.

I wanted this space to reflect me and mirror my personality. Fortunately, our bedroom held just the right corner. I envisioned a big, overstuffed chair placed diagonally in the corner nestled between two long windows that provided a beautiful stream of sunshine in the morning and access to gazing at the moon in the stillness of the night. I knew exactly what I wanted this imagined chair to look and feel like. It would be large enough for me to curl my feet under me and snuggle into the soft cushions it would provide. I scoured the internet looking for just the right chair, but each search yielded nothing. I shopped in brick-and-mortar stores tirelessly looking for just the right chair.

Finally, after exhausting all the avenues I could possibly think of, I called Penland's Furniture in Swannanoa, NC where we have purchased many home furnishings and asked if they could custom order a chair and have it made with fabric I would provide. Yes, was their answer!

I spent way more on the chair than I probably should have, but I was just a couple of years sober so I could always justify spending money on things that would last, like furniture or clothing, since I wasn't spending all that money on alcohol. I ended up calling the chair my "prayer chair" because it's where I spent time in prayer and time with God. (I've also been known to spend some time beside the chair on my knees as well.) It's the spot I go to write in my journal or sometimes I go there to have a good cry. I've mourned the death of my mother in that chair, cried over the letters I received from my son while he was in Basic Training thanking me for being there for him, and sometimes just quietly sat in that chair when the "Sunday Scaries" came. "Sunday Scaries" are precipitated by the "Monday Morning Blues." They are the feelings I have on Sunday evenings that leave me a little sad knowing the weekend is almost over.

Sometimes I've gone into my bedroom, slamming the door behind me when I needed to get away, because I was frustrated and angry at the world. I find comfort in knowing that I have one place in the house that I can go that's all mine. My husband and I joke about him not being allowed to sit in that chair. And while it is a joke, I'm very possessive of that chair, it really is MY spot. I think we all need a spot in our home that allows us to find quiet solitude in a busy and difficult world.

If you haven't carved out a special nook or room, or perhaps even a sacred place outside, I'd like to invite you to consider why that is. Especially when you're in recovery, retreat is necessary for restoration of the soul. When we've spent much of our lives living in an altered state due to being under the influence of a substance, much repair is often needed. Certainly, we recognize the need to mend relationships with family and friends, but part of real recovery begins when we can be alone and be at peace. This is why it is so important to have a place to retreat. We need to learn how to be alone with our thoughts and feelings without the numbing effects of alcohol or drugs.

Especially when you're in recovery, retreat is necessary for restoration of the soul.

Once your brain has grown accustomed to the stimulation provided by your chosen substance or behavior, you'll inevitably reach a point where alternative methods must be sought to fulfill that longing. In the realm of recovery, meditation and mindfulness emerge as two potent tools for self-care. These practices wield the power to alleviate stress, anxiety, and depression while fostering a comprehensive sense of well-being, thereby greatly aiding the success of your recovery journey. Comparable to coaching, both meditation and mindfulness entail cultivating an attentive focus on the present moment. By embracing these practices, you can enhance your mood, heighten self-awareness, and even pave the way toward achieving a more restful night's sleep.

For many individuals in recovery, me included, connecting to a higher power, who for me is God, is one of the most important parts of self-care. I discovered a totally different relationship with God in the rooms of AA. He was not the fire and brimstone God of my childhood. He was a loving God who had patiently waited for me to finally be done with drinking so He could fully show himself to me. God didn't just throw me a life preserver to save me. He jumped in the water, gathered me in His strong arms and pulled me out of a raging river that was drowning me. I can't tell you how many times He's met me in my special retreat in my bedroom.

Perhaps it's time for you to consider carving out a place that you hold as "your spot." Maybe it's not even a place in your home, but outside in the beauty and quiet of nature. It's time to learn to be ok with your own company. You might discover you're pretty fun to be with!

 **"Renovation Reflections"**

1. How have you created a sacred space for yourself?

2. What are you doing to connect to a Higher Power?

3. What healthy activities or practices have you used to replace your addiction?

Next: Make room in your recovery for the community of supporters who come and stay a while when you need them.

Chapter 11

Do Drop Inn

"In terms of recovery, it has been very important for me to be a part of a recovery community and to be around my people because they understand me actively. They get it."

~ Macklemore

Have you ever noticed in movies or TV shows, when a couple has a heated argument and one of them gets tossed out of the shared bedroom, the other who seems to be losing the argument always end up on the couch? It's typically not a one-bedroom condo or a NY studio apartment that this couple inhabits. No, this is usually a lovely duo living in a magnificent home complete with a grand entryway, huge chef's kitchen, multiple rooms, and a lavish owner's suite. But, somehow, someone ends up on the couch. Do these people not have guest bedrooms or a spare bedroom? Nope, we see the poor sap, dragging a blanket and pillow toward the couch, as they walk, dejected, from the bedroom. I know, now every time this scene unfolds for you on the big screen, you're going to remember that I pointed this out to you. You'll be whispering under your breath, "Just go sleep in the guest room! I'm sure that mansion must have a spare bedroom somewhere!"

But guest rooms were meant for that very thing, guests!

For years, I used my guest bedroom for the sleepless nights I endured due to my drinking. Alcohol may make you sleepy, but it does not make for restful sleep. There are numerous studies about the effects of alcohol on our sleep, particularly on our sleep cycle and REM (Rapid Eye Movement) sleep. This is the sleep we need for memory consolidation and emotional regulation.

When I drank heavily, I very rarely invited anyone over. Drinking, especially the amount that I drank and the person I became when I drank, was something I eventually kept secret. As my drinking increased, my desire to be social decreased. Alcohol became my prison. One of the many things I've enjoyed about being sober is the ability to have people over at any time and not worry about how I was going to be able to drink the amount of alcohol I would typically consume in a night. I don't have to wonder if my guests will smell alcohol on my breath when I greet them or count the number of drinks I have compared to everyone else.

When Gary and I bought the house in which we now live, one of the reasons we purchased it was the extra living space it provided. The downstairs is set up like an in-law suite and is perfect for hosting friends and family. Little did we know how quickly it would be used when we bought it.

As I recall, we closed and moved into our new home on a Friday in late June opening the door to a new chapter in our lives. A few days passed, and an unexpected situation arose when my younger sister and her husband found themselves in need of temporary accommodations. They had recently sold their own home much more quickly than expected and had not yet secured a new residence. We welcomed them into our home, offering the space downstairs for their stay. It was a delightful few months with them as our house guests.

A couple of years later, fate presented my sister and her husband with a similar predicament following the sale of their home. Once again, they found themselves seeking refuge, and approached us, inquiring if the "Roberts' Retreat" was available. This time, their entourage included their precious 10-month-old son. It was a remarkable experience to have a little one gracing our home, especially considering that Gary and I had not raised children of our own together. The laughter and innocence brought by their child's presence filled our household with warmth and delight, fostering an atmosphere of love and familial connection.

As the saying goes, good things often come in threes, and our home served as a sanctuary for my sister and her husband on not just one or two, but three occasions. Mirroring previous circumstances, they found themselves in need of temporary housing once again. Just like before, their family had expanded in size. This time, the growth included not only another child, but also a furry, canine companion. We reveled in their presence each time they graced our home, cherishing the laughter and love that filled the air.

The moments we shared during their stays were not merely temporary chapters, but cherished milestones in our collective story. Gary and I know the joy of hosting guests comes from the connections made and the sweet memories created. We've learned the best way to enjoy our guests is to give them space to relax and unwind. Having a place to share with friends or family is just one of the many things I enjoy about our home. The thing I love the absolute most about this home is that I've never had a drink in it.

Guest rooms are usually spaces that are prepared and set aside specifically for visitors. In recovery, it is important to create a community of support that is prepared and committed to supporting your new journey. This could be friends, family members, support groups, or even a healthcare professional.

We've learned the best way to enjoy our guests is to give them space to relax and unwind.

How might these individuals or groups support you? You may find an "accountability partner" to help you stay on track with the new goals you've set for yourself. They can keep you moving forward when you feel stuck. Friends and family members can offer emotional support, understanding, and encouragement as you navigate the challenges of recovery. Support groups, like 12-step programs, provide a sense of belonging and the opportunity to connect with others who have similar experiences. Healthcare professionals, such as therapists or counselors, bring expertise and specialized guidance to help you develop coping strategies, address underlying issues, and maintain your overall well-being. By surrounding yourself with this diverse network of support, you can build a strong foundation for your journey to recovery.

If you were going to create a welcoming guest room in your home, what would that look like? The redecorating or remodeling of the guest room might include things like ensuring the bed and bedding were fluffy and cozy, that there was a lamp beside the bed that provided soft, soothing light, but was bright enough should your guest decide they wanted to read in bed. (You know, if they decided that they wanted to read a book rather than scroll through their phone!)

You might make sure there was a phone charger and a sign in the room that provided your company with your Wi-Fi password. You would make the space warm and inviting in hopes your guests would feel comfortable and, most importantly, would want to come back. To me, hosting company is an opportunity to plant seeds of friendship that can grow deep roots.

Another aspect of creating a community of support for recovery is staying connected. Unless we simply didn't like the guests that stayed in our home, we would certainly want to stay connected with them after they leave. In recovery, especially early recovery, we need to stick close to our support systems. Whatever that looks like for you, whether it's attending 12-step meetings, getting involved in your local church, participating in online forums, or reaching out to friends and family, staying connected with others keeps you from feeling isolated and alone.

Just like you might have a plan in place for unexpected guests, like always keeping clean sheets on the bed or extra towels in the linen closet specifically for company, in recovery, you'll want to be prepared when you face triggers or cravings. You want to be equipped for any situation that may arise. For instance, if you know that you're going to be in a situation where alcohol will be present, you may want to have a sober support person on standby who you can call if you find the situation triggering.

Recovery doesn't need to be a journey you travel alone. Having a support system, whether one person or a group, may enable you to continue to carry on and overcome obstacles because you know you're not alone. Just like a well-appointed guest room, a community of support can provide comfort and encouragement, as well as a sense of belonging. Take the time to create and decorate your own community of support, and let it be a source of motivation and inspiration on your road to recovery. Don't wind up like that poor sap who is sleeping on the couch alone.

 **"Renovation Reflections"**

1. How are you treating the guests in your life?

2. What plans do you have in place for triggers or cravings to prevent relapse?

3. How have you connected with a community in recovery?

Next: Recovery requires cleaning up the messes you have made. And setting aside the time, tools, and place in your life for cleaning up the messes you will continue to make.

Chapter 12

Wash, Rinse, Dry, Repeat

"Our greatest glory is not in never failing, but in rising up every time we fail."

~ Ralph Waldo Emerson

The laundry room is certainly not the most glamorous part of the house, but it serves a crucial function. It's the place where we clean our clothes, our towels, and linens. It's where we send articles of clothing to get rid of the grime and grit of everyday life. Having a laundry room or at least a place for a washer and dryer is a must for most families. Just ask a mother of kids involved in sports the importance of regular access to a washer and dryer.

When we decide to renovate our homes, we usually start with the areas that need the most attention or where we plan to spend a lot of our time–rooms like the kitchen, the bathroom, or the living room. We want to make sure these rooms function well and reflect how we live our lives. Because the bathroom and the kitchen are often the costliest to renovate, we spend a lot of time researching and planning how to best proceed. We want these rooms to "flow." (We especially want the "flow" in the bathroom to work correctly!) Of all the rooms in the house, the one that is often overlooked in the renovation is the laundry room.

The placement of a laundry room in a home is also important. There are some people who wouldn't purchase a home if the laundry room were not in a location that suited them, like a laundry room in the basement of a two-story home, that's two stories above ground and one level underground. Who puts a laundry room in the basement and all the bedrooms on the second floor? I'm sure the decision to do so was based on the location of plumbing access. For some, the idea of a second story flooding due to an issue with the location of the washing machine outweighs the trek up and down stairs loaded down with laundry. Me? I'd take my chances with the laundry room located closest to where the loads are piling up!

My guess is that most new homes now include a laundry room. I was curious what percentage of new builds in 2022 included a designated laundry room in the home. And how might one find an answer to such a riveting question? Google it! Which is exactly what I did. Statistics with that information didn't immediately pop up but I was amazed at what did! Hundreds of websites dedicated to tantalizing topics like "Laundry Room Considerations" when building a home. Who will be doing the laundry? When will it be done, an important question due to the noise the appliances make? What kind of laundering will you be doing, heavily soiled clothing generated by children playing outdoor sports or just everyday clothing? Way more mental stimulation than I needed!

Renovating a laundry room in an older home will have its own set of problems and moving the location of the room might create even bigger challenges. Because of the pre-wiring and plumbing already in place, relocating the room may require re-thinking. A homeowner may want that laundry room out of the basement, but the home is hard-wired to have it exactly where it is.

Smaller homes may only have rooms for stackable units while other homes create elaborate laundry rooms that provide additional storage, the ability to iron in the room, perhaps a sink for soaking heavily stained clothes or to be used for hand washing delicates. I'm amazed at the number of Pinterest boards dedicated to laundry rooms. Admittedly, I have my own board with numerous pins of lovely laundry rooms. (I also created a board several years ago titled "When I have free time" which to this day, doesn't hold a single pin. I guess I'm not anticipating any free time soon!)

Laundry is infinite and it seems we never get caught up.

A laundry room is meant to be a functional space providing the homeowner with a place to wash and dry their clothing. That's really all it needs to do. A simple task intended to make our lives easier. The process of cleaning clothes and drying them used to be more of an event. In other countries, the task of washing and drying clothes is more detailed and takes up much more time–and yet it provides an opportunity for community among individuals. The invention of the washer and dryer and a room in our homes designated specifically for this task also can be a source of ongoing frustration. Laundry is infinite and it seems we never get caught up. After doing several loads of laundry and folding them on our bed, my husband will come into the bedroom and remark, "It looks like the bed vomited clothes." Personally, I don't mind doing laundry, but I don't enjoy putting clothes away. Similarly, I don't mind doing dishes but putting them away or emptying the dishwasher is not my favorite thing to do. (Do you see a pattern here? Perhaps you are one of those people I admire and "everything has a place, and everything is in its place." I am NOT one of those people.)

Sobriety is a lot like laundry!

At first, doing laundry may seem like a daunting task: the mound of laundry overflowing from the basket that was meant to contain it. Then it's the sorting, washing, drying, and folding that can all feel overwhelming. But the more we do it, the easier it becomes. We start to develop a routine, we create habits, we pick a day or two of the week to do laundry rather than doing a small load every day. After a bit of trial and error, we find a system that works for us. It's not so daunting anymore.

Sobriety is a lot like laundry! When we first get sober, our lives feel like a mess. What we've tried to shove into the proverbial laundry basket seems to have imploded and we don't know where to begin sorting. We see that we have damaged relationships, financial problems, or legal issues that need our attention. Each one of them is a separate but important pile. However, when we keep showing up, we dig through the piles, we start to clean up the messes we've made. We start to wash away the damage that addiction has caused.

We start getting the hang of this sober life. Wash. Rinse. Dry. Repeat. It requires repetition and work that is never ending.

Wash. When we first get sober, there is much about our lives that we need to clean up and wash away. Our past can be full of dirt and grime, and we know we don't want to carry these soiled parts into our future. We must determine how we are going to get rid of the stains and stench without ruining the garment itself. Are there areas of our past that need special attention and require pre-soaking to loosen the ground-in muck? Can we wash everything together or will we need to create piles that will be washed based on the necessary temperature of the water?

Rinse. After washing clothes, they need to be rinsed thoroughly to remove any remaining laundry detergent. In early recovery, rinsing involves removing any unhealthy thoughts or behaviors that prevent you from stepping forward into your new, sober life. Perhaps there are relationships that no longer serve you in a healthy way or hobbies you once participated in because they revolved around the substance of your choice. It's time to allow those patterns to flow down the drain, far away from you. It's a good time to consider adding "fabric softener" to the washing machine of life. This includes new interests and hobbies as well as learning new coping skills to deal with stress and the inevitable triggers that are a part of recovery.

Dry. "Dry drunk" is a term coined in the AA community that references someone who is no longer drinking but continues to exhibit the same negative behaviors they did when they were actively drinking. It is meant to describe someone who is physically sober but mentally still suffering with their addictive behaviors. In recovery from addiction to alcohol, we want to stay "dry" without being a "dry drunk."

This can be a challenging phase in recovery. You may feel like you've made great progress simply by no longer drinking. However, if you find you are struggling with raw emotions such as unresolved anger, resentment, depression, or anxiety, it may be an indication that you need to seek help to address these issues and learn new coping skills to avoid a potential relapse.

Repeat. Maintaining sobriety means continuing to do the necessary work. Recovery is an ongoing process. Just like laundry, we're never done. We need to repeat the behaviors that support our sobriety. It's not a one-time event. It requires commitment and willingness on an ongoing basis. When we stay on this path of recovery, we can create a life that is clean, healthy, and free of stains.

We need to repeat the behaviors that support our sobriety.

Getting clean from substance use disorder is truly like laundry. Wash. Rinse, Dry. Repeat. We don't have a choice in this if we're going to stay clean. Life can be messy, and we may find ourselves filthy some days. Fortunately, we know what to do because we're creating new habits. We know it's a never-ending process, but we've figured out what we need to do to stay on track. We've learned that if we repeat the behaviors that support our sobriety, it becomes easier. It has become part of our renovated routine.

"Renovation Reflections"

1. What piles of life's laundry need the most attention from you right now?

2. What does your recovery routine look like?

3. What benefits do you see in creating a healthy daily routine?

Next: Bright lights, mirrors, and grooming tools are necessary for the ongoing self-assessment required of us in recovery.

Chapter 13

Clogged

"The road to recovery is not a straight line. It's a winding path through valleys and hills, twists, and turns. But it's worth the journey."

~ Anonymous

Ask any general contractor which is the worst room in a house to remodel and without hesitation they will tell you it would have to be the bathroom. The older the home or the longer the bathroom has gone without any updates or upkeep, the worse the potential for a remodel nightmare. A bathroom, by its very design, is a conducive environment for incubating and growing stuff that is just simply gross. There's just no other way to say it but crap stinks. Unlodging a toilet or dismantling a tub often reveals years of undetected crud, filth, mildew, mold, and gunk. Gross, right?

My brother-in-law, Mike, shared another story with me about a bathroom renovation he was helping his daughter,

Maggie, with. She and her husband had purchased a "fixer upper" and they knew he would be able to help them with the "fixer upper" parts. Maggie had placed a bluing agent tablet in one of the old toilets thinking it might help make the toilet appear, if not at least smell, a little cleaner. A day or two later, after putting said bluing agent in the toilet, she noticed light blue rings beginning to appear on the floor around the base of the toilet. Not understanding exactly what was happening, she called her dad. He told her that the beautiful shade of light blue encompassing the porcelain throne indicated there was a leak somewhere. He came to her house the next day, pulled the toilet out, only to reveal a major rot problem in the subflooring. They were lucky they had not fallen through the floor based on the amount of rot he uncovered. What they thought was going to be a simple fix revealed a much larger and certainly more costly hidden problem that needed to be addressed.

Yes, plumbing is important!

Yes, plumbing is important! My family learned that lesson all too well with a water outage we experienced during the aftermath of Hurricane Katrina. Tyler was 12 years old at the time. At that stage in his life, he was not typically a consumer of water for quenching his thirst. He did, of course, acquire an immediate, desperate need for water as soon as he discovered we were without it and was convinced that he would surely suffer dehydration due to the lack of water no longer flowing freely from the faucets. I vividly remember him throwing his head back and in desperation clutching his throat with both hands saying, "Mom, I'm SO thirsty. I need water. I need water...now!" I can attest to the fact that thankfully, he did not suffer dehydration.

Plumbing allows our bathrooms to operate properly. Bathrooms provide us with a place to eliminate our waste, cleanse our bodies, and offer a well-lit spot for self-reflection–all with the capability of doing so in private. In our bathrooms, we strip down to nakedness–to our most vulnerable selves. We sometimes catch a glimpse of this nakedness in the mirror which, if we're not pleased with what we see, can lead us down a road of self-loathing and start a barrage of negative thoughts and emotions.

However, it's sometimes those very real reflections that lead to much needed solitary soul searching. The mirror reveals what we sometimes don't want to see or what we see and pretend is not there. I know this all too well.

It was the Christmas holidays, and Tyler was home on leave from the Air Force. I decided to host a small party celebrating him being home and as an opportunity to see friends we didn't get to see often. Whenever I plan a soiree of sorts, I swear to myself (and my husband), that I'm going to keep it simple. I am truly envious of people who host a party and make it look effortless. I'm not one of those people. Perfectionism and party throwing don't always work well together. Some people go to Sam's, Costco, Trader Joe's, or Whole Foods and pull together a party that is truly Pinterest worthy and never put a pot on the stove or a pan in the oven. Me? I feel like I'm in the kitchen for days leading up to the party because I think everything needs to be homemade. Which is exactly what I did for this gathering.

I made finger foods and dessert charcuterie boards. I believe Christmas parties aren't complete without Chocolate Crinkle cookies and Christmas Crack. Since these are my favorite treats, I decided to put several of each into a little plastic sandwich bag to be enjoyed later… and then hid them under my bathroom sink. (Yes, you read that correctly. I hid them!) I was ensuring I got my fill of the delectable desserts without stuffing my face with them during the shindig. After all, most people thought I was a very healthy eater who would never eat such sugar-laden sweets! Later that evening, after all the guests were gone, I quietly padded into the bathroom, gently opening the cabinet door, and proceeded to eat my treats in secret.

If we're not careful, we can easily trade one addiction for another.

As I savored those sweet treats, I caught a glance of myself in the mirror and sadly recognized the behavior. The mirror was only reflecting the truth I had been unwilling to see. My consumption of sugar had taken on the characteristics of my alcoholic behaviors! The woman eating those cookies behind closed doors was the same one that guzzled alcohol she'd hidden in her closet. It was a cathartic moment in my life–that's for sure. Addiction lurks everywhere in a variety of forms and sometimes we don't fully see it until it is staring us in the face like it was for me in that moment. I had replaced my addiction to alcohol with that of sugar.

If we're not careful, we can easily trade one addiction for another. And just like a toilet or drain that gets clogged, these addictions or addictive behaviors can slow, stop, or even back up our path of recovery.

For many women, the bathroom is where we refresh, renew, and get ready for the day. We shower, shave our legs, and wash our hair. Many of us then begin the careful ritual of expert makeup application. For some, it's a simple sweep of blush across the cheeks, a few strokes of mascara to lengthen stubby eyelashes and a splash of color on the lips and we're done. Others, it's a bit more in depth. Whatever steps we take, a few or many, it's an effort to enhance what we already have and to feel good about the person we see reflected in the mirror. (Thank goodness for Pinterest and Instagram influencers like Dominique Sachse who've helped me navigate makeup and skincare for a face over 40… or 50!)

Most men seem to be less fussy when it comes to getting ready for the day. Aren't they the lucky ones? However, their morning routine probably involves showering, shampooing, and shaving as well. Just like putting on makeup and preparing for the day, recovery looks different for each of us. It can involve a process of trial and error, trying different techniques and approaches until we find the look that suits us best. (I wonder if there are Pinterest boards addressing the various recovery techniques like there are for make-up?)

Before we leave this small but important room in the house, let's not forget the toilet! The toilet is probably one of the most crucial elements of the bathroom because it's where we relieve ourselves daily and then flush it away. Whatever we put into our body eventually makes its way out. When we enter recovery from addiction, we may find that we need to eliminate bad behaviors that no longer serve us or toxic people who are not good for us. They are clogging our progress and if not managed or eliminated, have the potential to cause some nasty problems. While we can't literally flush these things down a toilet, we certainly can flush out negative feelings and behaviors. This can be a painful, yet necessary process that we need in order to create new habits and healthy relationships.

Our bathroom of recovery offers a sacred space for self-examination, where we can pause, reflect, and reevaluate the choices we make. We cleanse and refresh our thoughts, allowing for growth and transformation to take place. The bathroom becomes a reminder that self-care and self-reflection are essential components of a newfound journey. It is a space where we can cultivate gratitude for the progress made, acknowledge the beauty of our evolving selves, and affirm our commitment to the path of recovery.

Whether the bathroom sheds light on old behaviors that are no longer serving us or provides the opportunity for us to see, perhaps for the first time, the beautiful person we are becoming as we carefully cleanse and refresh our thoughts, it's a necessary part of healthy recovery. We all need to visit this room daily!

 **"Renovation Reflections"**

1. As you look in the recovery mirror of self-reflection, what do you see now?

2. What "crap" do you need to eliminate from your life daily?

3. Is there anything that is currently clogging or backing up your recovery? If so, what can you do about it?

Next: When fear comes knocking at the front door, you need an exit plan – and comrades – you can rely on at the back door.

Chapter 14

The Thumbsucker

"Addiction is the only prison where the locks are on the inside."

~ Christopher Ferry

What's the first thing that comes to your mind when you think of a back door in your home? If you live in an apartment or condo, you may only have a front door. The way in is the only way out. Whatever and whoever comes into your living space must come through that one entrance.

Having a back door allows options. It allows for a quick get away from something or someone that may want to harm us. We see that all the time in the movies. Our hero is being chased, wanted for something he didn't do, and he ducks into the front of a business. In just a few seconds, the store owner surmises the hero is, in fact, innocent of whatever dastardly deed he is being unjustly accused of and points our hero to the back door. Of course, the back door almost always opens into a dark and dreary alley. The hero ducks into the shadows and waits for the villains to search for him in the alley, the dumpster, the turned over trash cans but it is to no avail. The villains throw their hands up in disgust when they realize they have been outwitted. They leave the scene and then our hero quietly slips out of his hiding place, a pleasant curve to his lips as he watches the bad guys leave the scene frustrated and empty-handed. All because of access to the back door.

The back door not only allows for an escape when needed, but it also is the entryway to the familiar. For many families, the front door is the formal entrance while the back door beckons to those who know us well. "Come on around to the back door–it's open" is what we tell our trusted friends. I love having backdoor friends! The kind of friends who know where you hide your spare key to the house. Who come in, take their shoes off, and if they want a cup of coffee or water, they feel comfortable helping themselves. And you wouldn't have it any other way.

The back door not only allows for an escape when needed, but it also is the entryway to the familiar.

One of my favorite childhood stories we would beg my mother to tell us repeatedly, is a perfect example of the unfamiliar coming to the front door!

My mother was the third daughter born in her family followed by a brother who arrived 18 months after her. She was born during the Great Depression and grew up in a family that didn't have a lot of extra money–especially with a family of four children. She often told us how poor they were and referenced her memories of getting oranges and underwear in her Christmas stocking and little else for gifts under the tree.

Her two older sisters were several years older and spent most of their time playing together, which left her to play with her younger brother. Since money was scarce, toys were not abundant. Fortunately, my mother was not short on imagination and could easily conjure up games for her and her brother to play that didn't involve the need for store-bought toys. One of their favorite games to play on Sunday afternoons was "church."

When my mother was probably about seven years old and her brother was five, they attended a small church in their hometown every Sunday morning. My mother would describe how the organist, while playing familiar hymns, would lean her head slowly towards the sheet music, while sitting on the organ's bench, then slowly lean her thin body far away from the music in a steady rocking rhythm. She continued the methodical motion throughout the entire song and my mother was mesmerized by it. After the final note of the hymn was played, the organist would lift her hands high in the air then slowly lower them to her lap, indicating the song was over and the preacher could begin. As the last note hung in the air, the preacher made his way to the pulpit to begin preaching.

Playing "church" for my mom and her brother consisted of her imitating the organist on their piano at home and her brother pretending to be the preacher. Of course, the movements of the organist as well as the passion of the preacher were both overly done by the two of them. I'm sure there was quite a bit of laughter exchanged between the two of them as their imagination and imitation grew with each passing performance.

Before I continue the story, there is an important piece of the story you need to know. My mother and brother, while different in many ways, shared a similar habit. They both sucked their thumbs. My mom told us her parents had tried everything they knew to try to get the two of them to stop. From bribes of new dolls and baseball gloves to coating their thumbs with some horrible tasting liquid, nothing curtailed them from this habit.

In a moment of desperation, her father stumbled upon a mischievous notion while perusing the local newspaper one evening. A prominent snapshot caught his attention on the front page of the sports section—an upcoming wrestler who was set to grace the town with his presence for a local event. Recounting this tale, my mother often depicted the picture in the paper as that of a perspiring, unkempt individual with unruly hair, evoking memories of the many faces sported by the wrestlers of the 1980s Worldwide Wrestling Federation.

With a pointed finger, my grandfather directed my mom and her brother's attention to the picture in the newspaper of the repulsive-looking wrestler, whom he dubbed "The Thumbsucker." He told them this ominous figure targeted children who were deemed too old to indulge in thumb-sucking, including the two siblings. (I must admit, it's rather dreadful to imagine sharing such a horrifying tale with a child! Although, I did once fabricate a story for my five-year-old son, claiming that we gave his mischievous golden retriever puppy, Buddy, to a blind man as a guide dog. The pup had a penchant for nibbling on walls! In reality, we found Buddy a loving home with a family friend who lived on a spacious farm, where he could frolic to his heart's content.) As you can imagine, my mom and her brother were gripped with sheer terror at the mere mention of this enigmatic character known as "The Thumbsucker."

It was just a week or so later, after the picture of The Thumbsucker had been pointed out to my young mother, she and her brother were charismatically conducting church services in the living room of their home as the early afternoon sun cascaded into the living room.

Knock. Knock. Someone was at the front door. No one ever came to their front door. No one except for strangers. Obviously, "stranger danger" was not a thing in the early 1940s. Mom stopped playing the piano and her brother ceased preaching mid-sermon so they could sheepishly answer the rapping at the door.

Slowly, they opened the door only to be struck with horror as they believed they had come face-to-face with the dreaded Thumbsucker. It was really her father who had borrowed an ugly mask that went over his head, covering his entire face except for his eyes. Of course, mom and her brother were so terrified when they saw the masked face, they both immediately registered the figure standing in the doorway as "The Thumbsucker" and he had surely come to get them, just as their father had predicted. (Again, I know! Even as I think about this story as I share it with you, I simply can't imagine the scenario. However, as I child, we loved to hear my mother tell this story!)

Knock. Knock. Someone was at the front door. No one ever came to their front door.

Mom's brother immediately ran and hid under a bed and my mother ran into the kitchen where her mother was washing dishes. She slid between the stove and the wall not far from the back door. "Libby," her mother exclaimed, "you look white as a ghost. What happened?"

"The Thumbsucker is here," she cried, "He's come for me and Buddy." She began to make her way towards the back door to make her escape.

Her mother wiped her hands on a nearby dish towel and walked to the front door to investigate what her two youngest children had seen. As she approached the doorway, she recognized the hands of the man standing there in the doorway as those of her husband and immediately began to scold him for scaring the two of them! He pulled off the mask, revealing himself to both his children as their familiar father. For my mom, the day the Thumbsucker came, the front door represented fear and the back door was a way out.

Is there a Thumbsucker at your front door? Things that look scary because someone else told you it was scary? Are you running out the back rather than facing what's at the front door? Have you allowed enough people access to your back door? Do you have friends now that know the songs in your heart and can sing them back to you when you've forgotten the words?

These are just some of the questions you may want to consider as you renovate your life in recovery. You get to choose your backdoor friends and face the fears at the front door.

Oh, if you're wondering if my mom and her brother stopped sucking their thumbs after that, the answer is no. My mother continued to suck her thumb until she was in the fifth grade. She said a cute boy told her that she was going to end up with buck teeth and no boy would ever want to kiss her. She said she stopped that very day!

"Renovation Reflections"

1. Who are your back door friends?

2. What fears are at your front door that you have not yet faced in recovery?

3. F.E.A.R. – False evidence appearing real. The Thumbsucker is an example of this definition of fear. What areas of your life are you inadvertently applying this to?

Next: Recovery requires insulation from the elements that fuel addiction and a space to work through new habits, relationships, and ideas.

Chapter 15

Where is Mrs. Ingles?

"I wasn't hurt by the fact that my "friends" weren't including me in on the action, but it was reality sinking in that I had no real friends that stung the most."

~ Kat Von D, *The Tattoo Chronicles*

I have a ghost in my house and her name is Mrs. Ingles. Apparently, she lived in the house before we bought it. Her primary place of residence is the attic. She doesn't appear anywhere else in our house, just the attic. It seems she has only appeared to my husband. We have dormer windows in the attic, and he says he's seen her in the window, sitting in her rocking chair with a bonnet on her head. Of course, Mrs. Ingles is a fictitious character created by my husband. I've yet to figure out why her name is Mrs. Ingles and why she is wearing a bonnet. But my husband is adamant about that bonnet!

Shortly after we moved into our home, Gary created this attic dweller, an aging woman named Mrs. Ingles. Apparently, she occasionally keeps him up at night with loud music playing and often complains to him when the temperature in the attic is less than she is liking. He hasn't told me the story of how she ended up in our attic or why she hasn't left. But we talk about her as if she is there. So much so that one day when I was mowing our front yard, I had this eerie feeling that someone was watching me from the dormer windows and looked to see if perhaps it was, in fact, Mrs. Ingles. Talk about a vivid imagination… even at my age!

The attic, in its traditional sense, isn't meant for day-to-day living and yet it has a very real and significant purpose. The attic is a very important, and often unseen, part of the function of a home. Attics are often used as a storage space for items that are used occasionally throughout the year such as seasonal decorations, out of season clothing, winter blankets and perhaps even sentimental items like old photos and scrapbooks. (As I write that word, "scrapbook," I'm thinking there may be generations of young people who have no idea what a scrapbook is, at least one that's not digital.)

Attics also serve as a buffer between the living space and the outside environment.

Attics also serve as a buffer between the living space and the outside environment. They are typically insulated which helps retain heat in the cold winter months and keeps it cool during the sweltering summer months. Mrs. Ingles told my husband it gets a little hot in the attic during the summer months and she wished he'd do something about that.

Often attics are designed to provide ventilation in the home, which helps regulate the indoor temperature and prevent the buildup of moisture. Without the proper ventilation, nasty mold and mildew can grow which can cause a whole host of problems for a homeowner. Sometimes, these are exactly the kinds of things that are discovered or uncovered during a home renovation project.

Just as a home needs an attic to provide insulation and ventilation, recovery requires the same. In active addiction, we may have inappropriately vented (read "yelled") when it was unnecessary and spouted untruths meant to be hurtful to protect our addicted selves. How many of us have remorse over the things we've said and done, perhaps even in a blackout state, that we wish we could undo. (Imagine an emoji with your hand raised!) That behavior and those feelings must find a safer way to be expressed and a better way to insulate ourselves from those that are perhaps not good for us or are unwelcome in our newly renovated life.

Just as a home needs an attic to provide insulation and ventilation, recovery requires the same.

There are many ways in which to "vent" feelings and perhaps one of the most helpful ways is that of journaling. Journaling gives you a healthy outlet for all the feelings and emotions you find yourself dealing with, perhaps for the first time in a very long time. Emotions can be overwhelming! A journal allows you to put pen to paper pouring out all those thoughts on pages meant for your eyes only. You can freely write about your frustrations with your friends or lament over your relationship with your lover. The best thing about journaling is that there is no judgment.

Journaling also allows you to see how far you've come in your recovery. If you choose to keep your journals rather than toss the pages after you've regurgitated your feelings on them, you can look back and see that you're learning to deal with life on life's terms. Let's face it, recovery isn't always rainbows and unicorns! There are days and moments when you're angry, upset, sad, or just plain miserable. A journal offers a place to download all those feelings and leave them there on the pages.

As you chip away at the life you once had prior to recovery and begin piecing it back together, you may find you need to ensure your own attic is well maintained. You may discover during an inspection phase of your life, whether it's at the beginning phase, middle, or even after you've built a solid life, that you now need added insulation. You may need to insulate yourself from people that could trigger a relapse. Perhaps this is one area of renovation that you may not have considered but could be monumental in creating a well-maintained life.

Insulation in the attic basically keeps the bad stuff out and good stuff in. How will you identify the good from the bad and what will you do with it once you do? What does that look like to you? Perhaps you are attending a 12-step program and surrounding yourself with positive, supportive people. You may have family and friends who have just been waiting for the opportunity to be part of this remodel and are ready to help.

But insulation isn't just about who you surround yourself with. It's also about what you do with your time and energy. Perhaps there are hobbies and passions you once enjoyed that active addiction robbed you of. You may even consider new hobbies.

In recovery, your attic space can provide a much-needed buffer between your past and your future. It's a place where you can store memories and emotions until you are fully prepared to deal with them in the present. It's where you can place your dreams for the future until you're ready to embrace them. In the privacy of your attic, you can reflect on your past and try to identify situations that trigger you and hold the potential to lead to a relapse. The attic can be a safe and supportive space, a buffer against negative influences and people that gives you the opportunity to sort through your past as you find a way forward.

The attic of recovery can serve as the perfect space for a fresh start, allowing you to rebuild and reboot your life. As you clean and organize the attic, metaphorically removing the cobwebs and dust of the past, you create a blank canvas ready to be filled with new and precious memories and experiences. It becomes a sanctuary of possibilities, a place where you can curate the chapters of your life that are yet to be written.

Enjoy this newfound space in your life. Just keep an eye out for Mrs. Ingles!

 **"Renovation Reflections"**

1. What are some new, healthy ways you're learning to vent your feelings in recovery?

2. What healthy buffers have you created between yourself and people, places, and things that could jeopardize your recovery?

3. How are you cleaning and organizing the attic space of your life?

Next: Addiction often includes hanging on to ideas and feelings and memories and relationships that support us in our worst behaviors, not in the new life we are creating. It's time to box them up and dispose of them.

Chapter 16

Love It or Lose It

"Your past does not define you, but it can help shape who you become.

~ J.K. Rowling

There is a world that existed pre-COVID and a world that now exists post-COVID, and some of it looks very different. No book written after March 2020 would be complete if it didn't include some reference to COVID-19. It was such a life-changing event for everyone in both big and small ways.

When COVID came, I was working at a hospital, but not in direct patient care and Gary was working for UPS as a driver. I knew he would be considered an essential worker and as it turned out, I would also be considered "essential." While this was a huge financial blessing, meaning that neither of us would have to quit work, it also meant we would be public facing amidst the fear of contracting COVID. Little did I know at the time how drastically my role at work would change to accommodate the needs of the hospital, or the impact making those changes would have on my view of what really mattered to me in my life. Like so many others, I began to question what was most important to me and whether I was doing what I felt I was meant to do.

I've often said my heart went out to those that were in early sobriety when COVID came. Being connected to a community of people through a 12-step program was the key for me in those early days of sobriety. Newcomers to AA are encouraged to attend 90 meetings in their first 90 days. If I were telling you this in person, I would use air quotes when I say the word "encouraged" and smirk. Ask anyone in AA about meetings and they'll respond quickly with one of their many sayings which is "Meeting-makers make it."

It was nearly 15 years between my first AA meeting and my last drink.

In early sobriety, those sayings drove me bonkers. They seemed so trite when my circumstances seemed so overwhelming. As time went on, I began to see that those little trite sayings would be the very words I would say to myself when I was tempted to drink. Trust me, there were a lot of times I wanted to drink. I wasn't one of the lucky ones that came into AA, picked up a white chip and never drank again. It was nearly 15 years between my first AA meeting and my last drink.

COVID took away all three of my most important self-care tools: church, AA meetings, and the gym. As the world adapted to the "stay at home" orders, we tried to re-create the things that were taken from us. Churches found a way to offer Sunday services online and AA meetings created virtual meetings. (I had a friend in AA that found a virtual meeting in Ireland and would join it just to listen to their Irish accents!)

Re-creating church services and AA meetings online presented a relatively manageable task but gaining access to a gym proved futile. After I attended rehab, I stopped drinking alcohol, but I had become a heavy consumer of the Kool-Aid of CrossFit! I was part of a community of people who worked out every morning at 6:00 am. (Ask anyone in the CrossFit community and they'll tell you there is a difference between the 6:00 am crew and the 6:00 pm group.) But how do you re-create a gym experience when not everyone has the equipment needed? Finding equipment during the first few months of the lockdown to outfit a home gym was practically impossible. Trust me, I know from firsthand experience. Gary drove me two and a half hours away from where we lived just to get three sets of dumbbells!

Exercise was a big part of my early recovery. Many people in recovery learn they need to replace their drinking with something else. A new habit and hopefully a healthy or less destructive one. I chose exercise.

I had been a member of a gym in the past but never really "embraced the suck" as they say, until I started doing CrossFit as part of my recovery journey. I personally believe CrossFit gained such popularity because it filled a need so many of us are striving for and that is a sense of belonging and community. I had been a member of a gym when Tyler was little and even had a personal trainer. I'd show up, workout with the trainer and I'd work out the other few days like I was supposed to do. However, I would also get in my car after working out and light up a cigarette. In the evening, I'd drink at least a six-pack of beer, sometimes more. I'd go to bed and do it all over again–day after day. Here, again, is another example of the life of lies alcohol helped me create.

I remember when I first started looking into joining a CrossFit gym. I was shocked at the monthly membership fee. However, when I did the math of how much money I wasn't spending each month on alcohol, I discovered the calculations were in my favor.

Here, again, is another example of the life of lies alcohol helped me create.

After all the times I'd joined a gym, trying aerobics, spin class, or other group exercise classes, I finally found something I really enjoyed and can honestly say I looked forward to every day. Ok, almost every day! It released endorphins that my body desperately needed. It was becoming part of who I really was. For so many years, I had projected the image that I was healthy while secretly participating in unhealthy behaviors. And I was beginning to embrace an authentic self and was becoming who I always wanted to be. Without fully realizing it, I was beginning my own renovation.

When my gym was forced to close because of the mandatory lockdowns required during the early months of the pandemic, I knew I needed to find a way to continue working out. I had a big enough garage that I could easily use half of it to set up the necessary equipment, once I found it. Setting up a garage gym created another problem. It required that I clean out my garage. Ugh!

If you're one of those people who have a neat garage, you may want to skip this part altogether! My garage was a catch-all for everyone's "stuff" and most of the "stuff" was mine.

The garage is where objects live until we determine, once and for all, we have no use for them. It's the same for many of our heartaches and hurts. We hold on to them until we finally realize how distracting they are for us as we try to become our best selves. At some point, we must determine it's time to let go of them. Often, during a renovation, the garage is where we move the unwanted or worn things to make room for new things.

To quickly make room for my much-needed self-care survival sessions, I just moved and stacked all the stuff to the other side of the garage, leaving enough space for me to workout. But each morning when I was working out, I saw all the disheveled array of assorted boxes and it was a bit distracting to me. It was hard for me to ignore them, but just as easy to not do anything about it. Morning after morning, month after month, I worked out looking at the mess, frustrated with it and knowing all the while how much happier I would be if I'd just take the time to do something about it. For whatever reason, the project seemed daunting and overwhelming. I'd have to make decisions about what to keep and what to get rid of. I'd need to weed out the garden tools and organize the array of car cleaning compounds! And what about the bikes, lawnmowers and weed eaters, oh my! You can see my conundrum, right?

Enough was enough! I made the decision to act! I went to the local hardware store, purchased matching plastic bins that would serve as storage for the items I determined to keep and heavy-duty trash bags that would be filled with the items that needed to be given or thrown away.

As I opened some of the very last boxes, I was shocked to find them filled with possessions I didn't know I still had.

Writing assignments from high school, pictures of people whose names I'd long forgotten, dishes I know longer used. So. Many. Things. I had moved these boxes from house to house, believing I needed what they held securely inside without even being sure what the contents were.

I wonder if you can relate to this in any way, if not in the physical sense of being what I think might be referred to as a pack rat, but in the metaphorical sense of keeping negative beliefs, bad habits, or toxic relationships that are no longer serving you–especially in recovery.

Perhaps you can pinpoint a time in your life when you began to consider making changes. A time when you came face to face with the unpacked boxes of past hurts, memories, challenging relationships, or unpleasant memories that you continue to carry with you. Occasionally, you find yourself staring at them in the corner of the garage, collecting cobwebs and simply taking up space and thinking it's time to do something with them. Even if we don't need the extra space for anything, why do we hold onto things that no longer serve us? What makes it so difficult to get rid of "stuff"?

Imagine the immense liberation that comes with releasing these long-held negative behaviors that have accompanied you, perhaps since your childhood. Picture the transformative experience of gathering all those thoughts that occupy valuable space within you and placing them in a 30-gallon trash bag, then confidently kicking it to the curb. By shedding this burdensome baggage, you create a spacious void that can now be filled with more positive and uplifting thoughts. The act of purging our past creates an indescribable sense of freedom, relieving us from the weight we carried by holding onto them.

As you bid farewell to these lingering negative remnants, a newfound clarity emerges. You become unburdened, enabling yourself to focus on personal growth, development, and the pursuit of becoming your best self. The release of these emotional attachments allows for a shift in perspective, leading to greater self-awareness, self-compassion, and the ability to embrace new opportunities and experiences with an open heart.

Just like renovating a garage to make space for new things, decluttering your inner world on this side of recovery has a similar effect. It opens possibilities for fresh beginnings, encouraging personal evolution and enabling you to build a foundation based on positivity, resilience, and self-belief. Embracing the process of letting go of your mistakes and fears of the past is an empowering journey that ultimately leads to a lighter, more fulfilling life.

So, take a moment to reflect on the incredible freedom and joy that awaits you by releasing the shackles of addiction. Allow yourself to envision the infinite potential that lies ahead as you create space within your heart and mind. Go ahead. Start clearing out the garbage in the garage and start making room for the new. Step forward into a future abundant with positivity, self-discovery, and unencumbered happiness.

 **"Renovation Reflections"**

1. What forms of self-care do you have in your life?

2. How are you getting rid of the wreckage of your past that no longer serves you?

3. Create a step-by-step plan to eliminate the unnecessary "junk" you continue to carry.

Next: Once you have transformed your recovery blueprint into an actual home, there's nothing left but to move in and make yourself at home – to begin a new life in a new house based on a solid foundation and strong support.

Chapter 17

Don't Waste the Waiting

"As human beings, our greatness lies not so much in being able to remake the world... but in being able to remake ourselves."

~ Mahatma Gandhi

Thankfully, at some point in a renovation project, you come to the end. You nail the last piece of shiplap into place. You put the finishing touches of a fresh coat of paint on the newly redecorated bedroom walls. You hang the final picture in a place that adds just the right pop of color needed. You take it all in, your heart filled with pride as you look around at a finished product covered in your fingerprints. Literally! Whatever type of repairs were needed, big or small, you reach the point where you sit back and sigh a little sense of relief because you've crossed the finish line of your remodel. It feels good! It's time to celebrate and let others see all the upgrades and improvements you've made. It's time for the "Open House."

An open house allows potential buyers a sneak peek at a residence they are considering as their new home. In the world of internet shopping, including real estate, it isn't until you set foot on a property that you get a sense of what it might be like to live there. All too often, a property that shows well online doesn't live up to how it's portrayed in the pictures. Wide angle camera lenses used by professional photographers enhance the appearance and size of the space. It may be difficult to gauge the ambiance, lighting, or even the overall wear and tear of the home. You can't experience the flow of the home or the layout until you walk through it. Of course, every home has its own smell, and until scent vision is created for online viewing, you won't know exactly what smells or aromas are wafting through the home without first-hand experience. (There's a reason why Realtors are encouraged to bake chocolate chip cookies prior to an open house!)

Welcome, dear friend, to the open house of your renovated life! Addiction held you in a dark, lonely place for so long, but now you are standing in the doorway of your remodeled and remade soul. There's light pouring in, illuminating all the results of your hard labor. It's a warm and inviting space, bursting with the potential of a fresh, new life. Step inside, take a deep breath, and soak it all in.

Welcome, dear friend, to the open house of your renovated life!

You might be feeling overwhelmed, even intimidated, by the newness of it all. You might be tempted to turn around and run back to the safety of your old, familiar ways. Growth doesn't happen without discomfort. Active addiction may have left you feeling slightly worn, somewhat damaged or completely broken. You may have felt like you needed a simple mini-makeover or a total remodel. Whatever the journey, how long it took you…you are here. This open house is an opportunity to step out of the darkness and into the light, to shed the shackles of addiction and embrace the freedom of sobriety. Your past need not define your future.

As messy and muddled as the process of a room or home renovation can be, rebuilding your life in recovery can feel equally scrambled. During the demolition stage, there is much disarray. Tools and materials scattered, walls torn down, paint splattered, and flooring ripped up. Your own rebuild may have felt painful, tumultuous, and never ending. However, you never lost sight of the plans. You pursued your new life with purpose. You didn't let the hiccups along the way hold you back. Now, you find yourself basking in the beauty of your new life. Look around. Who's there with you?

As a professional life coach, it is typically not my place to offer advice. A coach is meant to help you find the answers to your questions without giving guidance. I want to break that rule right now and share just a bit of wisdom from my own experience with you if I may. My one piece of advice is simple… Don't wait for the renovation to be over before you invite people in. Invite the ones you love to be part of the journey with you. Don't waste the "in-betweens."

As you move through the painful process of tearing down before you rebuild, take note of the people who want to be part of the process. You will find those that want to help you build a solid foundation. There will be those that want to work side by side with you, as you rebuild. Others will lift you up when you trip over the mess you've made as well as cheer you on when you succeed! Take the hands of those that genuinely offer it. Embrace those that love you even when you feel unlovable.

I have such gratitude for the people in my life who willingly stayed the course throughout the entire dusty and dirty path of destruction I created in my active addiction. Just the other day, as I was riding in the car with my husband, we were talking about someone we knew currently dealing with alcohol addiction. The destruction it was causing their life, the relationships being torn apart, and the inability of that person to see the devastating impact of their addiction on them and those around them. I reflected on my own active addiction days, specifically when I finally started seeing a therapist.

I had been seeing a therapist for several months and we had developed a good patient/practitioner relationship. In the course of our time together, she

Embrace those that love you even when you feel unlovable.

suggested it might be helpful for my husband to be part of the conversations. I thought that was a grand idea! If I'm being perfectly honest, I was hoping the therapist would help him understand how much of my issue with not being able to quit drinking was because of him. (Typical addict behavior–it's not MY fault!) Thankfully, she did not see it that way and helped Gary understand he was not responsible for my drinking. By allowing him to be part of that conversation, even though it wasn't what I wanted to hear, I was allowing him to be part of my renovation.

I thought about that conversation and how, at the time, I wasn't very happy with the therapist. It meant I had no one else to blame. I had to take responsibility. But, what a gift. If no one else was responsible for my drinking, it meant I had full control over whether I chose to do something about it.

It can be so difficult to let people in when all we want to do is hide. The question then becomes who are we really hiding from? Most of the time the answer is we are hiding from ourselves. We want desperately to not see the faults, the fears, and the fraud that stare back at us in the silent reflection of a mirror. If we can effectively deflect the negative consequences of our behaviors onto those around us, we don't have to accept the responsibility of making changes. If it's their fault, it can't be ours!

My husband and my son saw all the "in-betweens." Like it or not, they were part of my 15-year journey of falling and getting back up, repeatedly. Fifteen years of trying to get sober but continuing to drink. Fifteen years of being in and out of the rooms of AA and one trip to a 30-day treatment program. Fifteen years of the insanity of addiction. They saw it all and somehow continued to love me. They saw the good, the bad, and the downright despicable, but were there to see the beautiful restoration, as well.

When you create a welcoming, warm environment, build a strong sense of community, and share the progress you're making in recovery with others, you will find others asking about your blueprint. Who was your General Contractor? What tips can you provide them as they consider making their own repairs? Sharing your journey of rebuilding will help others create a vision of their own life of recovery.

In the coming days and weeks, as you settle into your new surroundings, you'll have moments of doubt and uncertainty. You'll wonder if you're on the right path, if you're strong enough to keep going, if you're worthy of this new life you've created. Know that you are all of that and so much more.

Welcome home! May you find in this new life all that you need for a life that is well lived. A life that is happy, healthy, and whole.

"Renovation Reflections"

1. What are you doing on a regular basis to ensure you're building a life that's happy, healthy, and whole.

2. What other parts of your life in recovery need renovation?

3. Who do you need to invite to be part of your "Open House"?

Next: Creating your own toolbox for recovery is possible.

Chapter 18

Building Your Toolkit

"Though no one can go back and make a brand new start, anyone can start from now and make a brand new ending."

~ Carl Bard

Addiction, like a wrecking ball, demolishes everything in its path, leaving behind a landscape of broken dreams and fractured relationships. But within the rubble, a glimmer of hope emerges, allowing you the opportunity to see what a life of recovery might look like. You realize the importance of arming yourself with tools to begin the restoration of your soul, as well as the rooms of your life that addiction has destroyed.

Now that you've taken a room-by-room walkthrough of what addiction and recovery can look like, it's time to consider how you can become a "DIY'er" for your own renovation. Many of the issues that we deal with in recovery are ingrained patterns of thinking, emotions, and actions that have led to self-destructive behaviors and unhealthy relationships.

Equipping yourself with the right tools to tackle these head on can mean the difference between living your best life, or merely a life of mediocre existence.

These character imperfections show up in a variety of ways, such as selfishness, dishonesty, resentment, unforgiveness, or fear, just to name a few. Addressing them is crucial to a healthy recovery. Just as renovating a house involves identifying and repairing structural or design flaws, addressing your character faults involves recognizing and learning how to transform your negative patterns of behavior and thinking to ones that serve you better in this new life you are creating. It's about getting unstuck and moving forward. It requires self-reflection, rigorous honesty, a willingness to change, as well as having the right tools and developing the skills to use them correctly.

It's about getting unstuck and moving forward.

"What are the most important tools a builder needs when they start a project?" I asked my brother-in-law, as I interviewed him for this book. "Well," he said, "which are you asking me about: the physical tools or the abilities of the builder?" Of course, I was asking about the physical tools, but then I had to consider his reference to the abilities of the builder. Without the proper knowledge of how each tool is to be used and the expert skills that are developed that come from regular use, the tools are merely implements without a skilled craftsman's hand to wield them.

As you begin to rebuild your life in recovery, you'll discover there are a variety of paths and multiple lessons to be learned along the way. A renovation project requires a plethora of tools. Your continued development will offer you access to an array of apparatuses that will help you tweak your recovery until it looks and feels like you. While you explore these new paths and develop the skills necessary to use some of the more intricate or complex gear you discover, there are a few that are considered standard.

The initial toolkit you assemble will consist of the necessary essentials and will expand as your recovery grows. It will take time and possibly the guidance of an experienced individual to help you acquire the skills needed to use these tools effectively.

A seasoned builder has often accumulated a whole host of tools that make projects much easier, especially tools that are used for more intricate projects. But to get started, there are a few essentials they need in their possession. Typically, the primary tools found in the builder's toolbox are a hammer, saw, drill, level, tape measure, screwdriver, and nails/screws. These too, will be the primary metaphorical tools you'll need in your own recovery toolkit.

Hammer of HONESTY

Admit we are powerless over (fill in the blank) with your addiction; that our lives have become unmanageable. Honestly admitting that we no longer have control over our addiction, or our lives, is the first step in the recovery process and often the hardest. It's what propels you towards a life of healing rather than imprisoned in a life of hell.

The hammer of honesty represents the enormous impact honesty plays in getting and staying sober. It symbolizes your willingness to break down the walls of denial and face the truth about your addiction, behaviors, and consequences. The hammer of honesty is essential in demolishing self-deception,

120

embracing your authentic self, and helping you lay the foundation for lasting recovery.

In the early stages of recovery, it may be tempting to minimize the severity of your addiction and downplay the toll it has taken on your relationships, your work, and your overall well-being. It's easy to want to forget the wreckage of your past, look hopeful at the present, and long for a future that is void of pain.

It's what propels you toward a life of healing rather than imprisoned in a life of hell.

However, when you grasp this metaphorical tool in your hand, you begin to clearly see the impact your addiction has on you personally as well as those around you. When used appropriately and skillfully, the hammer of honesty helps you confront the demons that haunt you. You recognize patterns of denial and acknowledge the impact addiction has on your physical, mental, and spiritual well-being.

A hammer, even in its simplest form, offers the builder a variety of uses. Its flat, level head is capable of driving nails into boards with just a few swings depending on the power provided by the person pounding it. If it's equipped with a claw opposite the head of the hammer, it holds the power to pull nails out of place. Sometimes, it is even used to break objects, materials, knock down sheetrock, or pry cabinetry off walls.

The hammer in your new recovery toolkit can be used to drive home your goals and aspirations. You can use your metaphorical hammer to establish firm foundations for your dreams. With each strike, you nail down your desire to create

121

a life of complete transparency. The power provided by your determination to live an authentic life fuels each swing, moving you closer to seeing a renewed sense of self. With every strike, you refine your character, chiseling away the unwanted aspects and revealing the true essence of who you were meant to be.

In addition, the claw of the hammer represents the power to extract yourself from harmful situations or toxic relationships. Like a builder uses the claw to remove nails, you can use your hammer to free yourself from destructive patterns and negative influences. With courage and strength, you can pry yourself loose from the grip of unhealthy habits and relationships, enabling you to create a healthier and more fulfilling life.

Your hammer also serves as a symbol of resilience and strength. It represents your ability to overcome challenges and rebuild your life. Just as a builder relies on a sturdy hammer to construct something new, you learn to rely on your inner strength and determination to rebuild your new life. The hammer becomes a testament to your resilience, reminding you that you have the power to rise above adversity and create a brighter future.

By harnessing the power of honesty's hammer, you unlock the ability to engage in candid and genuine dialogues, both with yourself and those around you. Through this process, you embrace accountability for your actions, enabling you to acknowledge errors and seek forgiveness when necessary. With integrity as your guide, you embark on a transformative journey of recovery, making impactful changes that lead to a splendid renovation of your life.

Saw of Self-Reflection

Just as a saw is indispensable in a carpenter's workshop, so too is self-reflection in the realm of recovery. With every pass of the saw, you inch closer to exposing your true self. The self you long to become. The saw of self-reflection symbolizes your relentless pursuit of cutting through the layers of denial that threaten to hinder your progress and opens you up to true self-awareness.

A builder's saw requires three crucial elements: a keen-edged blade, a reliable power source, and a steady hand. These three components form the trifecta for success. However, the absence of even one element can drastically alter the outcome, highlighting the interdependence of these factors.

Self-reflection often leads to an understanding of the importance of self-care.

Ensuring that you are operating with a sharp blade is crucial. A rusty, dull blade on your saw prevents you from recognizing and cutting through potential triggering situations that could lead to relapse. By acknowledging these situations, you make informed decisions and safeguard your progress. It's one of the first steps in carving a life of recovery.

Self-reflection often leads to an understanding of the importance of self-care. Exploring new ways to experience life can be both scary and exciting. You may try engaging in activities that rejuvenate the mind, body, and spirit such as exercise, meditation, or other creative activities. Establishing and adhering to a daily routine can play a pivotal role in breaking harmful patterns. Prioritizing adequate sleep and nourishing meals becomes indispensable on the path of sobriety. Each of these practices possess the power to fend off cravings and cultivate a positive mindset.

In the same way that a master carpenter expertly guides the saw through a block of wood, you must navigate the twists and turns of your own mind. It is through this careful handling of this savvy tool of reflection that you begin to dismantle the walls of denial that confine you. With each deliberate cut, you expose the raw truth beneath the layers of deception, enabling you to rebuild yourself with authenticity and integrity.

As you continue in your recovery journey, the saw of self-reflection allows you to see your newfound spirit. With each slice, you become aware of and confront obstacles that stand in your way. Triggers that once threatened to derail you become mere challenges to be conquered. Each swipe of the saw represents a moment of triumph, a testament to your progress and the strength you've gained on the arduous path of recovery. You may encounter moments of resistance when your saw seems to hit knots and tough spots that require extra effort. Recognize these obstacles as opportunities for growth and change.

Finally, the saw of self-reflection reveals a beautiful masterpiece beneath the surface. Through the challenges, setbacks, and triumphs, you are creating a life of recovery that is uniquely yours. The saw represents the transformation you've made as you navigate your triggers, while embracing a future of healing and personal growth. It symbolizes the resilience that lies within you and the strength you have cultivated to shape your own destiny.

By embracing the power of self-reflection, you become a master builder, reconstructing your life with intention and perseverance. With such a high level of self-awareness, you can navigate the intricate blueprint of your life, identifying the areas that need attention and renovation.

Drill of Determination

Recovery is a journey that requires unrelenting determination. The beauty of a builder's drill is that while it is one tool, the builder can adjust the speed with the amount of pressure on the trigger as well as the ability to use different bits based on the depth of hole needed or the type of fastener used. So too, can your drill of determination be used as a multifaceted tool of recovery.

Each bit at your disposal represents a specific opportunity for deep personal growth. You may be using the "bit of self-awareness" to help you determine what areas of your life you're paying attention to first. The "bit of ongoing support" might help you identify nurturing relationships with family, friends, or professionals that will provide you with guidance and encouragement. The "bit of learning" allows you to acquire new skills and knowledge about how to overcome obstacles. Each of these bits can be interchanged as needed.

Just as a drill bit must penetrate the surface to reach its target, you'll need to bore deep with determination to confront your challenges head-on and push past setbacks to uncover your true potential.

With the drill held tightly in your hand, you also have at your fingertips the ability to control the speed at which you approach each situation that requires your determination. In recovery, adjusting the intensity of determination is crucial. There may be moments where a slow and steady approach is needed, allowing you to carefully explore your emotions and aspects of your belief systems that continue to hold you back or that create obstacles that keep you from moving forward. A gradual pace ensures you can explore and examine these areas of your life without becoming overwhelmed.

In recovery, adjusting the intensity of determination is crucial.

There will be other times you will squeeze the trigger as tightly as possible, releasing all the torque the drill can provide. This is when a high level of unwavering determination is needed to break through barriers or shatter self-doubt. The relentless grinding of the drill symbolizes the struggle that accompanies personal growth, reminding you that change requires perseverance and resilience.

Renovations of the soul, much like renovations of a dilapidated house, demand unyielding effort and a steadfast spirit. The drill of determination, with its relentless rotations, serves as the tool that propels you forward on your recovery journey. It punctuates the process with precision, unearthing buried treasures of self-discovery and unleashing the potential that lies dormant beneath the surface.

The drill of determination proves that your true strength lies not in the absence of obstacles, but in your unwavering will to overcome them. With each triumphant rotation, it chisels away at the hardened walls, allowing you to embrace your vulnerabilities, and embrace the beauty of your imperfections.

Embrace the drill of determination. It symbolizes the power within you to break free from the chains that bind you. Heed its call, as it reminds you that the renovation of the soul is a symphony of strength, a dance of resilience, and a testament to the human capacity for transformation.

The Tape Measure of Accountability

An essential aspect of recovery is being accountable for your actions. The Tape Measure of Accountability serves as a reminder that you are responsible for your choices and the consequences that follow. It encourages you to reflect on your behavior, both positive and negative, and assess the impact it has on your overall well-being. The saying "You can't manage what you don't measure" holds true with recovery. By keeping track of your recovery efforts, such as attending support group meetings, therapy sessions, or engaging in healthy activities, you create a record of impressive achievements on your timeline of recovery. It also reveals areas of potential improvement.

As you continue to remodel your recovery, use your Tape Measure of Accountability carefully and thoughtfully, as real growth is achieved through ongoing measurement. You will learn to measure your progress not only in terms of your length of sobriety but the quality of the life you create. What are you doing to improve your character imperfections and to whom do you turn to hold you accountable? It's important to assess situations and relationships in terms of their potential impact on your recovery. Surrounding yourself with positive influences and avoiding triggers or negative environments can contribute to your overall well-being. Holding yourself accountable for the choices you make in terms of the company you keep and the activities you engage in is crucial for maintaining progress.

Your Tape Measure of Accountability can help you accurately set realistic goals. It will allow you to gauge your current abilities and determine goals that are currently within their reach, as well as set goals that may push you outside your comfort zone. The saying, "Start low, aim high" might be a motto you find helpful during this time in your life. Learning to set small, achievable milestones initially allows for steady progress, building momentum and confidence along the way. Setting unattainable or unrealistic goals may lead to frustration and discouragement which are potential precursors to relapse. You can align your aspirations with accountability to ensure your ambitions are grounded in a realistic assessment of your progress.

As you march towards your milestones with measured steps, it's important to remember that progress is not always linear. There may be setbacks or challenges along the way, but by using your Tape Measure of Accountability, you can reassess your goals and adjust them as needed.

By using this tool, you can measure your progress, set realistic goals, and work on improving your character imperfections. Remember to lean on your support system and seek the guidance of those who have walked the path of recovery before you. With accountability, self-reflection, and a commitment to personal growth, you can remodel your life and create a fulfilling future.

Level of Balance

In the journey of recovery, finding balance is crucial for maintaining stability and progressing towards a life that's happy, healthy, and whole. Just like a builder's level is used to ensure horizontal and vertical balance in construction, you'll need to seek balance in various areas of your life. Your level will allow you to access your emotional, physical, and spiritual well-being.

Your level will allow you to access your emotional, physical, and spiritual well-being.

One important aspect of balance in recovery lies in your personal relationships. The level in your toolkit allows you to distinguish between helpful and toxic relationships. Building healthy connections with others is critical for success in sobriety. It is equally important to recognize when a relationship is detrimental to your recovery journey. This can include relationships that enable destructive behaviors or fail to provide the support necessary for personal growth.

Achieving horizontal balance in personal relationships involves discernment and setting healthy boundaries. It requires the ability to differentiate between those who uplift and inspire versus those who drain and hinder progress. Just as the level ensures that a structure remains stable and even, you will need to evaluate each relationship in your life to ensure that it promotes emotional stability, personal growth, and sobriety.

The bubble in the builder's level extends beyond horizontal balance. It has the capacity to ensure vertical balance as well. Vertical balance in the recovery is measured in the context of a spiritual connection. Recovery is a deeply personal and transformative process that often involves a search for meaning and purpose. A spiritual awakening, in whatever form it may take, can provide a sense of grounding and perspective. It offers a vertical balance that can help align your values, beliefs, and actions which allow for a sense of harmony and inner peace.

As you explore your own belief systems and engage in practices that nurture your spiritual well-being, you'll begin to find your footing with a spiritual connection. Your new spiritual practices might involve meditation, prayer, mindfulness, or involvement in a supportive religious community. This journey can lead to a profound sense of inner peace, expanded consciousness, and a more meaningful engagement with the world around you. Embracing spirituality opens a doorway to explore the depths of your being and experience a profound sense of connection to the divine, to others, and to yourself.

The level serves as a powerful reminder for finding balance in your life of recovery. Just as the level ensures stability and harmony in construction, you will need to strive for balance in various aspects of your life. This includes horizontal balance in personal relationships, where one must discern between helpful and toxic connections, and vertical balance through a spiritual connection, which provides a sense of meaning and purpose. By embracing the lessons of the level, you can navigate life with greater equilibrium, resilience, and a foundation for a sustainable recovery.

Screwdriver of Self-Improvement

Like a skilled craftsman, you can use the screwdriver of self-improvement to dismantle destructive patterns and construct a foundation for a healthier and more fulfilling life. It symbolizes your willingness to make necessary changes, adjust your thoughts, behaviors, and attitudes, and fine-tune your approach to personal growth.

Just as you turn a screw, self-improvement requires your patience, focus, and a steady hand. You must confront deep-rooted issues head-on, fearlessly facing the forces that once held you hostage. Change cannot be strong-armed because applying too much pressure can strip a screw, making it nearly impossible to remove. No, the approach you take will need to be precise and methodical, making deliberate turns and adjustments as necessary.

You may try out a variety of methods to move you on the path of self-improvement. One such technique worth trying is "mindful meditation." Mindful meditation is a practice that involves focusing your attention on the present moment without judgment. This can be a valuable tool to support healing and sobriety. It acts as a soothing salve for a restless mind, guiding you towards tranquility and self-awareness. With each breath, you release the stresses and worries that entangle your thoughts, much like a calm current cleanses a riverbed.

You quickly learn "You cannot pour from an empty cup."

Journaling might also be a useful tool in helping unravel the tangles of your emotions and thoughts. It allows you to let go of the thoughts that have been holding you captive, offering a release from the mental clutter and emotional burden you may have been carrying. As you push the pen across paper or peck on the keys of a computer, you may uncover patterns, themes, or recurring thoughts that you hadn't noticed before. This level of self-reflection can lead to further personal growth, as it enables you to gain insights into your behaviors, beliefs, and values that are taking a new shape in your life of recovery.

You quickly learn "You cannot pour from an empty cup." Self-care is a vital aspect of the recovery process. Just as a screwdriver requires regular maintenance and care to continue to operate properly, you will need to nurture your mind, body, and spirit. Discovering and engaging in activities and hobbies that bring you joy and fulfillment becomes a top priority.

The Screwdriver of Self-Improvement becomes an important link as you rebuild your life in recovery. With deliberate turns and adjustments, you begin to embark on a transformative journey. When you take possession of this tool, you become an active participant in your recovery, taking ownership of your actions and choices. The screwdriver becomes a symbol of your commitment to self-improvement, representing the dedication and perseverance required to rebuild your life.

Nails of Resilience and Screws of Support

Just as the nails and screws are the fasteners builders use to hold together the varied pieces of a renovation project, so too are the metaphorical nails and screws that hold together a sober life. The "nails of resilience" and "screws of support" serve as the basic building blocks for a successful recovery. Just as a strong foundation is vital to any structure, these tools play a crucial role in renovating a stable and lasting life free from the grips of addiction. The nails of resilience and screws of support provide the strength and steadiness needed to navigate the challenges of the recovery journey.

Crafting a sturdy support system may, at first, seem like haphazardly cobbling together pieces of rubble that offer no real security or protection. However, with time and effort and careful consideration of each person you entrust a part of your recovery to, you begin to see a beautiful, welcoming space that offers more than you could possibly have imagined. A reliable support system is not only necessary but vital. Embracing the act of relying on others while offering your own support is like the twist and turn of screws, securing them into place as a builder does with utmost precision and care.

Resilience becomes the nails that hold the recovery process together, anchoring you to your commitment to sobriety. Just as nails can withstand external pressures, resilience empowers you to weather the storms of temptation and doubt. It is the unwavering determination that drives you forward, even when the path seems treacherous.

When the hard times come, and they always do, resilience will boost your belief that relapse does not have to be part of your journey. If it does occur, it doesn't have to derail or define your journey. Use it instead, as an opportunity for growth and learning.

Support systems and networks are vital in providing strength and guidance during challenging times. The screws of support serve as reminders that no one is alone in their struggle and that seeking help is a sign of strength, not weakness. You learn that surrounding yourself with a community that understands, supports, and encourages you on your recovery path is a must.

As you continue your journey of sobriety, remember the significance of your nails of resilience and screws of support. Resilience provides the strength to endure, even in the face of adversity, while support systems provide stability and guidance. In the construction of a successful renovated recovery, these tools are invaluable. Just as a well-built structure stands firm during life's challenges, a life built with the nails of resilience and screws of support forms the foundation of a sustainable, sober life.

Reinforcements - Putting It All Together

If you decide not to go it alone, a life or recovery coach can be a huge support by providing guidance, accountability, and motivation. A coach helps you identify your goals and create a plan to achieve them. This can include setting both short-term and long-term objectives related to various aspects of recovery, such as career, relationships, health, and personal growth. They can help you design and create your own blueprint for the remodeled life you seek and hold you accountable for the goals and milestones you set for yourself. They are also able to help you hone your skills with the essential tools needed for your recovery, as well as consider the additional tools you may want to add to your toolkit.

A life or recovery coach, especially one with lived experience, can provide support and encouragement. They can be a source of motivation, inspiration, and a positive outlook that helps you stay focused and committed to the renovation you are making.

The biggest role a coach has in your remodel is that of helping you identify and overcome limiting beliefs and obstacles that are preventing you from moving forward. A coach helps you identify potential challenges and develop strategies to navigate them effectively. They facilitate important self-reflection and promote self-awareness which allows you to develop new coping strategies, examine the beliefs that you hold to determine if they still serve you in your new life and help you discover new problem-solving techniques and resilience-building skills to integrate into your newly renovated life.

Just as a renovation project requires a variety of tools, your journey of recovery demands continuous growth and adaptation. It is vital to recognize that the initial toolkit you assemble is not exhaustive. As you progress, you may encounter new challenges or discover previously unseen character defects. In such instances, you must remain open-minded and willing to add new tools to your arsenal.

Just as a skilled builder can create renovations from raw materials, you will be designing a life of joy and purpose from the ruins of your past. With the tools now in your capable hands, you can reclaim your power, rebuild relationships, and rediscover renewal and restoration in your new life recovery.

Renovation is a process, not a static milestone. As your recovery extends forward, you will discover new needs, new resources, and new tools. Your growth may require an addition or renovation. With a solid foundation and the support of those who care, you are empowered to make your recovery home a reflection of your new life, new reality, and new possibilities every day.

Chapter 19

An Invitation

Dear Reader,

Congratulations on completing *A Renovated Life*! If you felt inspired by the principles shared in *A Renovated Life* and wish to embark on a more profound and individualized transformation, hiring me as your personal life coach or recovery coach can be the key to unlocking your full potential. Just as a skilled contractor can help a homeowner transform a dilapidated house into a beautiful, functional home, so too, can you renovate your life in recovery, one room at a time, with the help of a skilled professional.

As your personal life coach, I will walk alongside you on your journey, providing unwavering support, guidance, and accountability. Whether you're seeking to overcome personal challenges, improve relationships, or rediscover your passions, I will help you navigate the path to growth and self-discovery. Together, we will explore the metaphorical rooms of your life, identifying areas for improvement, and implementing practical strategies to achieve your goals.

For those on a recovery journey, I understand the unique challenges and triumphs you may face. As your recovery coach, I will be your ally, helping you maintain sobriety, build resilience, and reclaim a life filled with purpose and joy. My approach is rooted in compassion, empathy, and evidence-based techniques, ensuring that you receive the personalized support necessary for lasting recovery and well-being.

By hiring me as your personal life coach or recovery coach, you will benefit from the following:

- **Personalized Guidance:** Receive tailored guidance and support, focused on your specific needs, goals, and aspirations.

- **Accountability:** Stay on track and motivated as we work together to set and achieve milestones, ensuring progress towards your desired outcomes.

- **Empowerment:** Develop a deeper understanding of yourself, your strengths, and areas for growth, empowering you to make meaningful changes in your life.

- **Overcoming Obstacles:** Learn effective strategies to overcome obstacles and setbacks, building resilience to face life's challenges with confidence.

- **Sustainable Transformation:** Embrace long-lasting positive changes that will extend beyond our coaching sessions, impacting all areas of your life.

- **Safe and Non-Judgmental Space:** Share your thoughts and experiences in a safe, confidential, and non-judgmental environment, promoting healing and growth.

- **Support for Recovery:** If you're on a recovery journey, benefit from my expertise and personal experience with addiction and recovery, ensuring you have the tools to maintain sobriety and well-being.

- **A Trusted Partner:** Experience the power of having a dedicated and understanding partner committed to your success and well-being.

Whether you seek personal growth, recovery support, or both, I am here to guide you on your path to a renovated life—a life filled with purpose, fulfillment, and a renewed sense of self. Remember, just like any renovation project, lasting change requires effort, but with the right coach by your side, you can overcome any obstacle and create the life you've always envisioned.

But why stop there? What if I told you that the principles outlined in this book don't just apply to your personal life? What if I told you that your organization, too, could benefit from a renovation – a renovation of its approach to addiction and recovery in the workplace? Imagine turning your workplace into a "Recovery Friendly Workplace," where employees thrive, teams unite, and productivity soars.

Transform Your Workplace with a Recovery-Friendly Remodel

Workplaces have traditionally been viewed as separate from personal struggles and challenges, but the truth is, our personal and professional lives are interconnected. By creating a Recovery-Friendly Workplace, you'll foster an environment that values wellness, promotes empathy, and empowers employees to bring their whole selves to work.

As a life and recovery coach, a nationally board-certified health and wellness coach with a background in human resources, and the author of *A Renovated Life*, I stand ready and eager to help your company unlock its true potential. Allow me to share a blueprint for why hiring me as your keynote speaker, workshop facilitator, or recovery consultant will be the best investment your organization ever makes:

- **Renovating the Workplace Culture:** Just as a remodel starts with a solid foundation, transforming your company's culture is the cornerstone of a Recovery Friendly Workplace. I can guide your leadership and HR teams in creating a supportive and stigma-free environment, encouraging employees to seek help, and fostering an atmosphere of empathy and understanding.

- **Increased Productivity:** Just like a well-designed kitchen, a recovery-friendly workplace optimizes workflow and boosts productivity. By supporting employees in their journey towards recovery, you create a space where they can thrive, resulting in enhanced focus, creativity, and engagement.

- **Stronger Teams:** Think of your team as a room in need of renovation. By prioritizing communication, fostering empathy, and implementing recovery-supportive policies, you build a foundation of trust and unity. A united team is like the perfect blend of colors on the walls—a harmonious masterpiece.

- **Retention and Recruitment:** Much like a house with irresistible curb appeal, a recovery-friendly workplace attracts top talent. By showcasing your commitment to employee well-being and providing support throughout their recovery journey, you'll create an environment that people can't wait to be a part of.

- **Reduced Stigma:** Just as a freshly painted wall can brighten up a room, a recovery-friendly workplace helps combat the stigma surrounding addiction and mental health. By openly discussing these topics and providing resources, you'll create a culture of acceptance and understanding.

- **Cost Savings:** Remodeling can be an investment, but it pays off in the long run. Supporting employee recovery helps reduce absenteeism, turnover, and healthcare costs, while increasing overall job satisfaction and employee morale. It's like discovering hidden gems behind the walls—rewards you never expected!

- **Recovery Support Systems:** Imagine the workplace as a well-designed room with tools within arm's reach. I will work with your organization to install recovery support systems, providing employees with the resources they need to flourish. From workshops to group coaching sessions, my metaphorical toolbox is filled with strategies for success.

- **Navigating Through Challenges:** Just like renovating a house, there may be unexpected challenges along the way. As a seasoned recovery coach, I know how to navigate these obstacles, providing your employees with the tools to handle stress, setbacks, and maintain resilience.

- **Remodeling Personal and Professional Development:** A renovated life is a journey of growth, and your employees' personal development will have a direct impact on their professional success. Through 1:1 life and recovery coaching, I will empower your team members to discover their true potential and contribute even more significantly to your organization.

- **Creating Harmonious Teams:** In any renovation project, teamwork is essential. By facilitating team-building workshops, I can help your staff develop a sense of camaraderie, ensuring that every team member plays their part to the best of their abilities.

- **Unlocking the Hidden Potential:** In every renovation, there's always untapped potential waiting to be discovered. As a coach, I specialize in helping individuals identify their strengths, talents, and passions, allowing them to bring their best selves to the workplace.

- **Adding the Finishing Touches:** A renovated home is complete with the finishing touches, just as a Recovery Friendly Workplace is adorned with compassion, support, and appreciation for its employees. Together, we'll polish the environment, making it a place where everyone feels valued.

However, what truly sets me apart is my personal experience with substance use disorder and recovery. My journey to sobriety was made possible by one of my previous employers, igniting a deep passion within me to help other organizations create recovery-friendly workplaces. This desire to pay it forward fuels my dedication to this cause.

So, dear reader, perhaps it's time for you personally to take the next step–to embark on this transformational journey together. Whether you seek personal growth, recovery support, or both, I am here to guide you on your path to a renovated life–a life filled with purpose, fulfillment, and a renewed sense of self. Remember, just like any renovation project, lasting change requires effort, but with the right coach by your side, you can overcome any obstacle and create the life you've always envisioned.

As an organization, hiring me as a keynote speaker, workshop facilitator, or recovery consultant will breathe new life into your organization. Just as *A Renovated Life* has provided you with metaphorical tools for personal growth, I am here to furnish your company with the tools for success.

Let's create a workplace where addiction and recovery are approached with understanding and compassion. Together, we'll remodel your organization into a Recovery Friendly Workplace, where employees thrive, teams unite, and your company's future is transformed.

Wishing you a beautifully renovated future,

About the Author

Kit Roberts is a speaker, author, consultant and certified life and recovery coach. She's a self-proclaimed life enthusiast, professional problem-solver, and all-around supporter for those seeking their best life.

With a toolbox full of expertise, lived experience, and a flair for DIY (Do It Yourself) life transformations, Kit fearlessly tackles the topics of addiction awareness in the workplace and helping employers become recovery friendly. She's gifted at crafting work cultures that can withstand any renovation challenge. Whether your office needs a fresh coat of employee engagement, sturdy foundations of wellbeing, or a complete makeover in recruitment and retention, Kit has the tools and know-how to get the job done.

When she's not wearing her corporate toolbelt, she's helping individuals and groups create blueprints for a life that's happy, healthy, and whole. She loves helping her clients navigate obstacles and demolish those pesky limiting beliefs. Watch out for those "ah ha" moments—once you have one, you'll never be the same again!

Ready to get started? Visit her at www.arenovatedlifellc.com to discover the incredible range of services she offers. Grab your toolbelt and start building something amazing together! Just remember, bring your sense of humor and a healthy dose of enthusiasm—Kit doesn't do boring, and neither should you!